DAVID G. RETTIG

UNSUCK IT!

A Candid, Humorous, Systems-Thinking Look at Business & IT

ISBN 9781691849017

Dedication

This book is dedicated to my wife, Missy Rettig, and my mentor, Greg Schuth.

Missy, without your encouragement and support I would have never gone into the career that I love. You've put up with me working 12-hour days, then coming home and staring at the laptop for 6 more hours. You've put up with over a decade of grad school. You've taken care of the kids while I traveled, regularly gone for weeks and once for nearly half-a-year, so that I could do the job I love. You deserve a better husband than I am. I love you.

Greg, you are the best leader I've ever had. You were my first, best example of everything a leader should be. The first time we met I was so belligerent and insubordinate, you should have fired me on the spot. Instead, you said, "You don't know it yet, but I'm going to be your best friend." You were right then like you usually are. My career and my life would be completely different had I not met you. You have my unconditional respect and love.

I owe both of you everything that I am professionally.

To my mom, Teresa Reiter, who and demonstrated a work ethic that I've strived to emulate.

To my children Benjamin, Charlie, and Rebecca, affectionately called The Spawn, I am so proud of each of you. You are better than me in so many ways. Remember the family mottos: Be Wonderfully Weird, Normal is Boring, and Never Choose to Be Average.

To my friends who walked with me through the battlefields more than once: Cameron Ames and Dean Maglinte. Thank you for making being a leader easy.

And finally, to the people who modeled real leadership by giving me their time: Guillermo Diaz, Katty Coulson, Lance Perry, Mark Campbell, and Michael Quesada. Thank you for pushing me to be better than I am.

Love and Respect, David

I really worked here.

The server room of a $100M+ company when I started.

CONTENTS

PREFACE / PG-RATED

A month ago, I released this same book with a more provocative title and a smattering of profanity. Like 160+ F-bombs. A smattering. Seriously, that's less than 0.6% F-bombs. I think the FDA allows a higher percentage of bugs in peanut butter.

But some people were put off by the profanity. Including Amazon advertising who told me: "Your book title or cover contains profane terms. To ensure a good customer experience, we do not permit profanity in any form, including obfuscated or abbreviated terms." This version is a PG-rated version of that book. The title rhymes if you feel like you want the grittier version. Other than profanity, the content is the same.

Now for the PG-rated version of my earlier title. Enjoy!

Some people struggled with a I imagine this book is going to make a few people angry. You may be reading this now, thinking, "You're right, dude. I'm angry right now."

If you're an angry IT person, you're thinking, "This guy is going to blame IT for everything, just like everyone else does."

If you're an angry non-IT person, you're angry because you found out that I don't blame IT for everything. I'll quote a great man, who once will have written,

> **"It doesn't matter** who caused your broken IT. Blaming someone doesn't fix it. Blaming the department or leader does not fix it. Whether it's the Business People's fault, the Geeks' fault, a combination of both, or the gremlins' fault, because Zach Galligan can't follow three simple rules, **it doesn't matter** and **knowing who to blame doesn't** make it better**. You just want to fix your IT, right?"
>
> David G. Rettig, *UNSUCK IT!*, p.32

Do yourself a favor. Set aside your anger. Read this book. Think about the stuff that makes you angry. Ask yourself: does it make you angry because it's wrong or does it make you angry because it's right?

This is not a finger-pointing book. This is a solutions book. If you are looking for a book to help you find out who to blame, you might be the problem.

Let me leave you with one more thought. A definition of a very important word that I'll use throughout this book.

Sucks [suhks]

Adjective

1. Broken. Ruined. Not achieving the intended purpose. Failing to function well.
2. in a difficult or hopeless situation.

When I say, "IT sucks," I mean both ways.

Therefore, when I say, "Unsuck IT", I mean:

Unsuck [uhn-suhk]

Verb

1. Fix. Achieve the intended purpose. Function well.
2. Treat fairly. Appreciated. Give hope.

Do you want to fix IT? Me too.

ABOUT THIS BOOK

This book is not about fixing your technology. I'm not going to talk about a specific technology <u>at all.</u> Because technology changes all the time. The same problems have existed for decades. The first great book on enterprise-level software development, *The Mythical Man-Month*, examined the problems with large software projects... in 1975. Over 40 years later, we still have the same problems.

Because IT is about People, not about technology. Most IT problems are not technology problems. Most IT problems are people problems.

I wrote this book so that Non-Technical People and Technical People can understand and benefit.

This book avoids technical lingo because the technological lingo sometimes used by IT People exacerbates the divide between IT People and Business People. I **hate** it when IT People expect Non-Technical People to learn about technology. I **hate** it when IT People laugh at Non-Technical People behind their back for not understanding technology. (Trust me. They do. Search for "stupid user stories" in your favorite search engine, if you don't believe me. On behalf of all my fellow Geeks, I'm sorry.). I **hate** it when IT People use technical language to get Non-Technical People to go away or sign a PO so they can get some new toy. I **hate** the us-vs-them attitude that has become the de facto culture of IT. I **hate** it so much that I wrote this book.

We need to work <u>together</u>, or this situation is never going to get better.

You should also be aware that **this book contains a smattering of sarcasm**. For sarcasm, I will use a special font. This one. The one you are reading right now. The same font I use throughout the entire book.

Occasionally, I will write about a technical concept. Not a specific technology. Not bits & bytes. Not pieces & parts. But a concept. When I talk about a concept, I will put it in *italics* and define it in parenthesis immediately following the word. I'll also call it out in a shadowbox beside that section. I promise that this book is completely free of *geek-speak* (the lingo used by IT People that no one understands).

For the sake of brevity (and because I am too lazy to keep typing it), going forward this book will refer to *IT People* as "Geeks" and *Non-Technical People* as "People" or Business People. If you are a Geek, know that I call you "Geeks" with all the love in my heart. I am a proud geek. My best friends are Geeks. My 16-year-old son who-I-love-more-than-my-own-life is an all-caps GEEK. Being a geek has paid my bills and sent me to college and grad school. I do not consider "Geek" a derogatory term.

WHY DO I CARE WHAT THIS GUY THINKS?

I've been in IT and IT leadership for a long time. I sold my first computer program in 1981 but didn't start a professional career in IT until much later. I was that geeky-neighbor that you brought your broken computer to. You know the guy. You keep him as a friend because you don't want to pay your local electronics shop $100 an hour to remove a virus you got from that completely not-porn-website. Sometimes he looks at you like you're a moron when you can't connect to your wireless, but he fixes it, just to have another human to talk to. Yeah...I was that guy.

Then in 1996 or 1997, my wife got sick of having her house full of broken computers and told me to try to get into IT. I worked hard to get some *IT certifications* (a "driver's license" for a specific technology.)

Since then, I've been working in IT and IT leadership for over 20 years. I've led teams at Fortune 500 companies with over 100 Geeks and small businesses with 3 Geeks and everywhere in between.

IT Certifications

A "driver's license" for a specific technology. You can drive without a driver's license, but if you want to find out if someone has been trained to drive, checking their driver's license might help.

THE EPIPHANY

A long time ago, I was the senior Geek for a $200M company. I had built the company's email system (I had built everything) and the email was breaking nearly every week. I met with the owner of the business and explained the problem (using my best Geek-speak) and everything I had tried to fix the problem. Then I asked for $5,000 for a new piece and part. He replied, "David, you just don't understand the business."

I left his office distraught, head hung low, obviously wearing my failure and frustration on every inch of my body. I met my boss's boss, Greg Schuth, as I walked out of the owner's office. Greg saw my defeat and asked what was wrong. I recounted the story of my frustrated attempts to fix the broken email for the low price of $5,000. Greg said, "Wait here", walked into the owner's office, and closed the door.

Five minutes later, he walked out and said, "I got you $50,000. Fix the email." My jaw dropped. Up was down. Black was white. Everything I knew was wrong. When my head stopped reeling, I said, "You know something I don't know. I need to know what you know." That was the moment Greg Schuth became my friend and mentor and I realized that my technical knowledge was worth exactly zero. That was the moment, I started on the path that gave me over a dozen years of fixing broken IT departments, usually starting with a phone call, "David, can you help me? My IT is broken..."

IN THE BEGINNING...

CHAPTER 1: IN THE BEGINNING...

I'm sick of silver bullet solutions. **Silver bullet solutions offer a simple fix to complex problems.** Business bookshelves are full of quick fixes. A quick search produced over 50,000 titles with quick fix offerings. Some common silver bullet solutions are:

- Drink eight glasses of water a day and lose weight!
- An apple a day keeps the doctor away!
- Eat oatmeal to cure heart disease!
- Vote for my favorite politician!
- Chew gum to stop smoking!
- Build a baseball field in your cornfield.
- Set up a website and your business will grow!
- Eat dinners together and your family problems will go away!
- Mine cryptocurrency and you'll be rich!
- The 5 secrets of successful people!
- Implement Agile and your software development will be fast!
- No, DevOps is better!
- Wait...what about Kan Ban?
- No, Scrum!
- Scrum is part of Agile!
- This software will make you secure!
- Do this 5-minutes a day you'll be a great leader!
- Throw the ring in the volcano and the evil wizard will die!

Silver bullet solutions do two things really well. Sell books and extend the problem. While you're trying the silver bullet du-jour, the problem still exists.

Silver bullets are attractive because they are easy and fast. **We like fast and easy solutions.** As a lifelong fat-guy, I can tell you no fat-guy wants to hear, "I can help you be thin and all it will take is rethinking everything you do, everything you eat, everything you believe about food and exercise, and possibly some of your relationships." I want someone to give me a pill that will make me lose 150 pounds and let me eat an entire box of Pop-tarts every meal. And don't come at me with that six-pack of Pop-tarts... I want the family-sized.

This isn't another silver bullet solution.

This book is a candid, holistic overview of why IT is broken and how to fix IT.

The guidance in this book <u>will</u> fix your IT. But it won't be a quick, easy fix. It will take rethinking everything you do, everything you believe, and possibly some of your relationships.

This book is laid out in three major sections. We start with examples of broken IT in Section 1: Tales of the Broken. Then I present the reasons behind the broken IT in Section 2: Why is This Happening. Finally, in Section 3: Fix It, I show you how to fix things. You may be tempted to jump to Section 3. It's your book; do what you want, but I wouldn't recommend it. Section 3 refers to concepts in Section 2. Section 2 refers to scenarios in Section 1. You could just ahead, but it's a short book. Suck it up and read it.

Let's get to fixing things.

SECTION 1: TALES FROM THE BROKEN

CHAPTER 2: WAR STORIES

After a particularly terrible day, Geeks will congregate at their favorite ice cream shop for a hot-fudge sundae and commiseration, to share their latest tale of woe. As the empty sundae dishes stack, like a bunch of old fishermen, the IT stories get more and more fantastic, just like the size of the fish. Geeks call these "war stories".

In grad school, the texts contain tales of stellar successes, fabulous failures, and bumbling blunders of companies. We tell stories because humans are tribal creatures and for millennia, we have learned through stories told around the campfire. Despite the glow of electric lights replacing the campfire, we still learn best through stories. Grad school texts call these "case studies".

My war stories of a few of the broken IT departments that I've unbroken. Call them case studies, if you prefer the more clinical term, but let me tell you, in the midst of the story, it feels like a war.

I hope these stories enable you to see that you aren't alone. Your IT department is broken or else you wouldn't have bought this book, but so is almost everyone else's. Hopefully, you'll leave this section seeing some of your current situation and think, "We have the same problems. Maybe this guy can help." I hope you'll also leave this section shocked at some of the war stories and think, "Gosh. We aren't _that_ bad." If you don't think that at least once, I'm glad you bought this book. Seriously. Take the rest of the day off, finish this book, and then let's get fixing... because things aren't going to fix themselves.

By the way, I've changed the names and some of the non-essential details (including company descriptions, revenues, and functions) to protect these organizations, the people, and myself. The essence of every story is completely factual and not exaggerated at all.

War Story 1: The First Professional Geek

A \$250M+ sales and service company's IT department consisted of a young Geek fresh out of college, a friend of the owner, an accountant who liked computers, a data entry clerk from another company, and an IT manager who showed up four hours a day then hid in his office. I was the company's first Professional Geek hire. The first Geek to have a few of those IT certifications, any real training, or any experience with enterprise IT. The current Geeks did the best they could, but without any real training, they didn't know what they didn't know.

That IT department was broken. Things crashed all the time. Every day at lunch, the IT department shut down everything. If they didn't, everything started crashing around 3:00 PM. The company ran on an old *UNIX green screen system*. (If you don't know what that is, thank God for your luck. It would make you sad.)

UNIX GREEN SCREEN

If sadness could be a computer system, it would look like this. Imagine your computer came attached to your solar-calculators' screen. About like that.

The UNIX system did text-only email. No pictures. No attachments. No calendars. No contacts. No fonts or colors. Text. Two or three times a day, someone would enter a wrong number in the UNIX order taking system and the entire order taking system would just die for the entire company. IT would have to call the one guy who wrote it to get it working again. A quarter-billion-dollar company depending on one guy and he was a four-hundred-years-old (that might be an exaggeration). Usually once a week, all the printers connected to the UNIX system stopped working for a really geeky reason that none of the current Geeks knew how to fix.

Speaking of printers, the orders would get printed on triplicate paper (one white sheet, one yellow sheet, and one pink sheet). The company paid a person to separate the triplicate and put one in the old-style bank carriers that suck through a vacuum tube to the factory. The person would then <u>scream</u> into the PA system, "ORDER UP!" A dozen times a day, with every order, everyone in the entire office would hear the raspy screech of "ORDER UP!!!" None of the Geeks saw this as an IT problem.

The company was on three floors and, with each ascending floor, the internet got slower and slower. Really. First floor, okay internet. The second floor, kind of bad internet. The third floor, God help you. Needless to say, all the VPs were on the first floor. The current Geeks didn't know any better. That's just the way things worked.

Upstairs there was a big cage full of IT junk that the manager refused to throw away because "someday we might need that". He asked me to find something to do with all of his junk. Somehow magically compost a bunch of trash into something valuable. Luckily... I mean, unfortunately, all his trash mysteriously vanished one evening... they never found the guy who disposed of three pallets full of *hard drives* (all smaller than 500 *MB*), *BNC network cards*, and *dot-matrix printers*.

Hard drives, BNC cards, and dot-matrix printers are *geek-speak* for old junk. Junk you couldn't give away in a free box in a garage sale. Junk Goodwill wouldn't take as a donation.

WAR STORY 2: A GEEK HOARDER

This company was a shining example of corporate glam. Glass desks, bright colors, clever slogans on the walls, an entrance foyer filled with lush greenery, a dark wood half circle desk, and a pretty receptionist. Everything was meticulously groomed for the visiting customers which included government officials, military officers wearing stars, and CEOs of multibillion-dollar companies.

Except IT. The senior Geek of this department had a hoarding problem. The Geek had a massive server room with a pile (a literal pile) of junk in the middle of the room. Finding anything took hours as he dug through this heap of manuals, disks, electronic bits, old cables, new cables, tapes, broken computers, monitors, and keyboards. Hundreds and hundreds of keyboards. Luckily... I mean, unfortunately... the new guy had a relationship with an electronics recycler who could haul away pallets of junk.

In all seriousness, the Geek returned from vacation after the CIO and I had hauled out two large dumpers full of junk for an electronics recycler. The Geek started crying when he came back from vacation and saw his pile of junk gone. Crying. Over. Junk.

Now that's broken.

_____

One evening, a former co-worker called complaining about her IT Director at a Tier-1 Automotive Supplier. The current IT Director kept telling her that IT couldn't do anything that the business requested. I gave her some ideas about how to approach some of the technical problems.

The next day, she called back. She fired the IT Director and offered me his job.

That IT department was broken. The email was on an out-of-date system because the current Geeks didn't like Microsoft. The company didn't have wireless because the current Geeks didn't think wireless was safe. The CEO couldn't use his iPhone because the Geeks didn't like Apple. One-third of the IT budget went to support the former IT Directors pet project, an expensive, overpowered *ERP* (an application that combines most of the business functions into one big program).

The network security guy wouldn't give remote access to anyone except himself. Not even the CEO. The IT department had set up some wonky system that logged everyone out of the internet every 30-minutes. The CEO and VPs would be in the middle of a webinar with a customer and half-an-hour in would get kicked out.

ERP

An ERP combines most of the business functions into one monolithic program. People who sell ERPs will tell you they are the best thing since sliced bread. Most Geeks will tell you that the ERP that they know is the best ERP (which guarantees them a job). Most Business People dislike their current ERP, but don't know how to get out

They had a <u>large</u> office filled with old manuals and disk that no one would throw out, fearing that someday someone would need something that they had pitched. All the desktop computers came from an online auction site for $10 each and would crash randomly throughout the day. When someone needed to turn off their computer, it took 30 minutes to turn it back on. One Geek was taking the company backup tapes to his garage because he wanted "offsite backups in a safe place".

My first day on the job, the president of the company said, "I moved IT to the building out back because I'm sick of looking at their faces." Gosh. That's broken.

War Story 4: CEO Says Hop on One Foot

I had joined a technology training company with over 100 locations throughout the U.S., served over half-a-million customers, and made billions annually. A vendor with whom I had worked previously was the account rep for my new employer as well. When he heard that I left to work with this new company, he said, "Dave, I know you fix broken IT departments, but this place is so broken... I don't think even you can fix it."

Hold my beer.

When I started, the Geeks that I led received over 15,000 emails a day from computer systems telling them systems were broken. A literal 15,000 emails every 24 hours. One geek sat at his desk watching one customer-facing website all day and restarting the computer when the website went down. The Geeks were on-call 24x7 and had to be available or risk termination. The Geeks wanted to make things better but didn't have a minute to spare from dealing with crisis after crisis.

All decision-making went to the CEO. Literally all. I managed over 100 people and, when I attempted a $10 purchase, I was called on the carpet for not sending through the right approval channels. A manager couldn't spend $10. My boss, the Director, couldn't authorize $10. His boss, the VP, couldn't authorize $10. The VP's boss, the CIO, couldn't authorize $10. My $10 request went to the desk of the CEO, where it was promptly declined. Batteries for remote controls in the meeting rooms needed to be checked out. Once, I asked for a box of pens and was told by the office manager that I could have, "...one pen. You don't need more than one pen at a time." At a profitable, multibillion-dollar organization... one pen.

But the control didn't just apply to finances and resources. I wanted to swap two of my employees' assigned seats to facilitate cross-training.

When I asked my boss, he said he would run it up the chain. Several days later, I got a rejection email from the CEO.

The Geeks managed support through a cumbersome application that made doing their job three-times as difficult. Everyone in the organization knew this application was a hindrance, but the CEO belonged on the board of directors of the company that made the application. I was told that that app was "untouchable".

One afternoon, a CFO I had previously worked with invited me out to lunch. She had changed jobs again and was the CFO of a mid-sized international nonprofit and the IT department was broken. She asked me to come to fix it. It was a smaller organization than I typically helped, but the CFO was a friend, and my current company was over the worst of their problems, so I took the job.

The company was built entirely on some homebrewed, custom application that made clients jump through dozens of hoops to do anything with the nonprofit. For example, the client had to print a PDF, hand fill out the PDF, scan and email the PDF to a staff member, who then entered the data into the client tracking application. The Geek *developers* (application creators) controlled all the reports from the system and would not give anyone access to the data in the system. If finance needed a report, IT would run the report and email the output to finance a couple of days later. If finance needed the same report a month later, the Geeks needed to run it again. The Geeks didn't even trust the People to run the reports themselves.

The Geeks had put locks on the doors to the IT department and during business hours, locked the door. They had put a sign on the door with a cartoon Geek saying, "GO AWAY! IMPORTANT WORK HAPPENS HERE." When asked about serving the People working for the nonprofit, the Assistant IT Director said, "My responsibility is data integrity, not taking care of them." I couldn't believe my ears.

The People who worked at the nonprofit preferred the Geeks behind their locked doors. The only time that the Geeks talked to them was to tell them they weren't allowed to do something that they needed to do for the customer or the nonprofit.

The president of the nonprofit was so frustrated that he contracted a "smart IT guy he went to college with" to recreate everything the current program did. The smart guy had charged the nonprofit $5M over a year and shown no results to date. Not one thing.

A professional friend and recruiter called me, saying, "I found the perfect job for you. This place is broken." The CIO called the recruiter and the recruiter knew my rep.

The CIO used to be a software developer Geek. She got promoted by default and wasn't really trained or equipped to lead. Fortunately, she recognized that she needed help, but had failed to grow anyone on her team to help her. When the CIO contacted the head hunter, he called me.

During the first interview, the CIO asked me what the first thing I change. I said, "I don't really know. I need to observe the department. Find out what's broken before making a bunch of changes. I don't have a silver bullet solution." She said, "We wanted someone to come in and shake things up."

The team consisted mostly of software developer Geeks, who had written nearly every one of the 500+ applications that the company used, ranging from simple time tracking apps to insanely complex engineering apps. The CIO had written many of these applications herself, before being promoted. Whenever a new problem arose, she saw an opportunity for the team to create yet-another-program.

Now, the team was so busy maintaining the myriad applications they created that they couldn't deliver anything new that the company needed. Many of the home-built applications talked to one another; therefore, whenever the Geeks did give the company something new, half a dozen of the other applications would break.

The Business People saw the department as an expensive bunch of Geeks unable to meet even basic business needs. The company, once on the bleeding edge of technology, was now a laggard, years behind their competition. The Business People ramped up their demands, hoping that the team would perform.

When the Business People asked why the department failed to deliver value the CIO blamed the Geeks for not working hard enough. She started demanding more hours, mandatory unpaid overtime, and mandatory weekend. Even when the CIO heard that the team was overworked, she didn't believe it and asked the team to start reporting how many hours a day they worked and on exactly what they worked on.

The CIO insisted the Geeks release the software on time, even if it meant the software contained bugs. To meet the demands of the CIO, the Geeks needed to cut out non-essential things like documenting anything or testing the software. When the business received the software, it would break their systems, resulting in days or weeks of rework.

The CIO started hiring expensive external consultants to create new applications to meet the needs of the Business People. Then she would tell the Geeks to support the new applications because the external consultants were too expensive to keep supporting what they wrote.

The Geeks were demoralized. They felt like the CIO didn't support them. They knew their reputation with the business. They knew that the software had a reputation for being buggy and barely functional, but they blamed the Business People for not giving them the time or staff to fix the old programs. They wanted to create new applications for the business but saw all the interesting jobs going to pricey consultants.

Fortunately (or unfortunately), the company paid well-enough that the situation was tolerated. The CIO usually hid in her office with the door closed, coming out only to issue some new demand on the team. Between the infrequent appearances of the CIO and the company's pay, the Geeks hung in there, hoping for a light at the end of the tunnel.

How do these war stories strike you? Believable? These are all real problems, faced by real businesses and real IT departments, real People and real Geeks. I can still feel the pain these organizations felt. I still remember the hopelessness. It's all so wrong and so common.

Most Business People report that they have no idea what their Geeks do. Most People report that their IT departments are not a competitive advantage, do not add to the organizational value, and do not equip the business to take advantage of new business opportunities. Ouch.

I **hate** that People see Geeks that way because the Geeks I know desperately want to help. That's why they got into IT. They like to use technology to make things better.

In Section 2, we look at common themes of these war stories to build the foundation for fixing your IT in Section 3.

SECTION 2: WHY IS THIS HAPPENING?

CHAPTER 3: NINE REASONS IT'S BROKEN

We just looked at six war stories from my past. Trust me. There are more but I think these six represent a far overview of the issues that most businesses and IT departments face. In this chapter, we review the types of problems in the war stories, the causes of each of these problems, and the consequences of the problems.

We will also talk a lot about value in this section. It's important when you read "value", you know exactly what I mean. I've spent a lot of time in lean manufacturing environments and I like the Kaizen definition of value: **value is anything that your customer will pay for.**

> Value [/ˈvalyo͞o/]
>
> *Noun*
>
> 1. Anything your customer will pay for.
> 2. That's it. Sorry, buddy.

Some Geeks like to argue that their customers are the Business People and if the Business people say, "We want it" then it must be valuable. I don't see it that way.

Geeks are employees of a company, just like every other person in the company. The company has one customer: the customer. The people who buy and pay for the company's products: whether that's pampoogas, pantookas, or drums!

If the company's customer would buy more pantookas through an iPhone application, then an iPhone application adds **value**. If an iPhone app is nifty and everybody in the company thinks we need to do it, but the customer doesn't care, the iPhone app does not add value.

If something doesn't add value, you <u>cannot</u> stop doing it. Geek friends, don't run to your boss and say, "David Rettig's book said to turn off all the firewalls." Because I did not say that. Business People friends, do not slam my book down on the CIO's desk and demand that he gets rid of all the printers because printers don't add customer value.

I'm saying that when I talk about value, I specifically mean "anything the company's customer will pay for".

We will get to why creating value is important…critical…almost oxygen for fixing IT in Section 3.

PROBLEM 1: BLAME (OR UNDERSTANDING) DOES NOT FIX THE PROBLEM

I was in a fleabag hotel in some tiny town, traveling for business. I had just finished a 12-hour day, just wanted to crawl into a pool of ice cream sundaes, and sleep a few hours, before doing it all again, when one of the supervisor's reporting to me called: his team (my team) had released a new application with a bug that caused a six-figure error (over $100,000 error).

I called my boss. He needed to know about the problem, so when he got a call from his boss, he wouldn't be blindsided. I calmly explained the situation, what we were doing to fix it, and controls that we would put in place to ensure this didn't happen again.

My boss hissed, "Who did this?"

I replied, "I don't know. I didn't ask. The team staying at the office until it's fixed. I'm going to log into the *war room* with the team until it's resolved." A *war room* is an all-hands-on-deck emergency meeting that my teams use to resolve critical problems.

My boss demanded again, "Who did this?"

I replied, "I don't know. I didn't ask. It doesn't matter. If you want a name, if you want someone to blame, you can blame me. I did it. I'll take the bullet. I'm not going to let some witch hunt distract the team from fixing the problem."

After 10-seconds of silence, my boss said, "Fine. I don't need a name. Get it fixed."

> **War room**
>
> An all-hands-on-deck emergency meeting that my Geeks use to resolve critical problems. For remote teams, a war room can be virtual (Webex, Teams, GoToMeeting, Slack, whatever). For Geeks in one location, it was a literal room.

33

The point of that story: **This section (and this entire book) is <u>not</u> about blame.**

To quote the preface of the brilliant book *Fix IT*, "**It doesn't matter** who caused your broken IT. Blaming someone doesn't fix it. Blaming the department or leader does not fix it. Whether it's the Business People's fault, the Geeks' fault, a combination of both, or the gremlins' fault, because Zach Galligan can't follow three simple rules, **it doesn't matter** and **knowing who to blame <u>doesn't</u> make it better**. You just want to fix your IT, right?"

(How 'bout now? Mind blown? I just created a circular reference. What did I write first... the preface quoting this section which quotes the preface or the other way around... holy moly... it's quotation inception...)

Business People blaming Geeks or Geeks blaming Business People has become the de-facto culture of many organizations with broken IT. I don't know if it's a cover-your-butt environment or a lack-of-ownership or bad leadership or cowardice, but we can fix it. But that's section 3.

I guess I need another caveat here: **I'm not abdicating consequences**. If you accidentally swallow cyanide instead of cinnamon, you die (consequences). If an employee messes up repeatedly (or even extremely badly one time), sometimes they get fired (consequences). Does it matter <u>why</u> you swallowed cyanide instead of cinnamon? If your neighborhood poison store (you have those in your neighborhood, right?) mislabeled the cyanide as cinnamon, you are still dead. If your wife switched the labels, you're still dead. Finding out who to blame doesn't fix the problem, but there may still be consequences. If you're in leadership, you take the blame for the problem and you might face the consequences for something that you didn't do. Stop whining. Suck it up. That's why you have the big-boy or big-girl desk.

In War Story 3, the CEO blamed the entire IT Department. In War Story 6, the Business People blamed the Geeks, the CIO blamed the Geeks, and the Geeks blamed the CIO and the business People.

CONSEQUENCES OF BLAME

Blame is toxic and has terrible consequences. Blame turns divisions, departments, co-workers, spouses, and friends into enemies. Blame destroys morale and productivity. Blame reinforces the us-vs-them culture that is so pervasive in IT.

You need to kill that attitude toot-sweet. Section 3 will address that.

I once sat on a conference call where every time the Business People asked for something a Geek would say, "That's really hard." Afterward, I called the Business People and said, "I'm afraid whenever a Geek says, 'that's hard', you hear, 'my job is harder than your job'." The Business People said, "That's exactly what I hear." Let me preface this section by saying, I'm **not** saying that at all.

Everyone has a hard job. To me, my mechanic has a hard job. I don't know anything about cars. The gas goes in the hole in the back and the key goes in the hole in the front. End of my car knowledge. When I take my car to my mechanic and say, "I put the key in the hole and it doesn't go", my mechanic doesn't respond, "I'll fix it, but that's really hard." If he did, I would say, "If it was easy, I would do it. That's why I'm paying you instead of learning to do it." Actually, I would <u>think</u> that not say it, because I still need the car to go and if I piss off my mechanic, we won't fix my car. (BTW... my mechanic is awesome. Thanks, Brian & Leo for keeping my Mustang running.)

In summary, I'm not saying IT is harder than your job or any job.

Now that I've thrown up all the caveats... someone once said, "Everyone thinks they can write a book because everyone can sign a check." The Geek corollary of this is "Everyone thinks they can be in IT because everyone has a computer at home." War story number 1, 5, and 6 have elements of "Anyone Can Do IT" in them.

In War Story 1, the IT department was staffed by IT people without any real experience in IT. In War Story 5, the president of the nonprofit hired some guy he knew to circumvent his IT department. War Story 6 is a little different. The company promoted a Geek to Head of IT. War Story 6 is anyone can be a leader.

Think about your current job. Did you hit the ground your first day able to do your job at the same skill level you have now? Have you gotten better over time? Have you learned some tricks that make you qualitatively better? I'm not talking about just faster, but better. Have you developed an almost sixth sense about some aspects of your job? Of course, you've improved... or you better have! People get better with practice. There are things that you did on the first day of your career, your first month, your first year, that you look back on and think, "I'd never do it that way again."

Geeks face the same limitations. There are things that you learn over time that make you qualitatively better at your job. Day one, you might do things one way, but after a year, you learn that way has all sorts of problems, so you change it. Here's one minor difference: Geeks tend to work on the <u>same thing</u> over and over.

I don't mean the same <u>types</u> of things. I mean the <u>same</u> thing. Let me clarify by helping you visualize a little bit.

Imagine that you build houses for a living. When you first start your job, you build simple box houses with four walls and a roof. That's where your skill level is. Eventually, you grow in skill and you can build more and more complex houses with two different roof planes, split levels, and increasingly unique styles. After years and years, you master your skill and now you can build amazingly complex structures with brilliant form and function, like Frank Gehry's Walt Disney Hall in Los Angeles.

Now imagine that you build <u>one</u> house for a living. When you first start your job, you build a simple box houses with four walls and a roof. As you grow in skill and you <u>can</u> build more and more complex houses with two different roof planes, split levels, and increasingly unique styles, but you can't tear down the simple box house you built because <u>the people who pay you</u> are living in it. Instead, you try to apply some of your new skills to the box house. You make it a little better here and a little better there, but the box house was never designed to support what you can do now. After years and years, you master your skill and now you can build amazingly complex structures with brilliant form and function, like Frank Gehry's Walt Disney Hall in Los Angeles. But you still have the box house you started with; a box house can never be turned into the type of structure you should have built if you would have had the skills you have now. In fact, you can't build what you need to build because of what you did when you started.

The second example is how Geeks work. A Geek creates a program to help the business. They do the best they can with their skills year one. The business uses the program and year two asks the Geek to make the program better. The Geek has the skills to create a <u>much</u> better program, but they are limited by the program they made year one. Year three, the Business People need even more functionality out of the program and the Geek doing exactly what they need, but not to the program they are using. If they could just tear it down and start over... but that would be... really hard...

When a Geek says, "That's really hard", he or she may not mean "my job is really hard," but many times they are saying, "The program you need me to change was never designed to be used that way. I'm not sure I know how to change it in a way that will work."

CONSEQUENCES OF INEXPERIENCE

How does this connect with "anyone can do IT"? If you start with inexperienced Geeks, your company might end up with a technology foundation equivalent to a box house; it will work for now, but in the future, any changes will be really hard. You may also end up with simple technological issues that an experienced Geek can fix, like the printers failing in War Story 1, but an inexperienced Geek has no idea how to approach. Lastly, you may not know what you don't know. Again, in War Story 1, the Geeks had no idea that there were other options for email. They didn't know that they shouldn't have to shut down the systems in the middle of the day to keep everyone working. They didn't know that the order entry systems shouldn't crash willy-nilly. They didn't know that the internet didn't get slower as you when up the steps. That's the way it had always been done.

PROBLEM 2A: ANYONE CAN DO LEADERSHIP

War Story 6 included a CIO who was pushed into a leadership position for which she wasn't ready. This is the essences of *The Peter Principle* (a theory explaining how we end up with bad managers). This is not going to be a chapter explaining the Peter Principle.

The Peter Principle

The idea that when you are good at one job, you get promoted into a new job which you might not be as good at. Wash, rinse, repeat, until you end up in a job that you are incompetent at. This explains how we end up with bad managers.

I don't believe in a natural-born leader, just like I don't believe in a natural-born racecar driver. Driving a car is a skill. Leading people is a skill. The difference is, despite the most excellent movie *Talladega Nights: The Ballad of Ricky Bobby,* no one tells one of the pit crew to jump into the middle of a race and take over. But we do this stuff to Geeks and People all the time.

We say, "Here you go. Here are the keys. Lead this group of people" with absolutely no training in leadership. That's insane. Stop doing that to people.

Leaders <u>matter</u>. **Have you ever worked for a bad leader?** Remember how they made you feel at work every day? Remember how you felt Sunday night because tomorrow was Monday and you had to see them again? Remember how you felt after work? You came home drained, exhausted, angry, spent. You didn't have anything left to give your wife or kids or dog. How did that affect your wife? Your kids? Your dog?

That bad leader just made your family's life worse and they didn't even know your family.

Have you ever worked for a great leader? Remember how they made you feel? Remember looking forward to doing your job because you knew you mattered and what you did was important? Remember everything you learned from that leader? Remember the amazing things you and your team did? A great leader helps you achieve more than you ever thought you could. A great leader helps you grow and helps you advance and opens new career possibilities.

You come home energized and excited about your job. You are a better spouse, a better parent, or a better fur-parent because of that great leader, and they didn't even know your family.

Maybe that leader encourages you to return to school. Maybe that leader gives you stretch assignments. Maybe because of that leader you move into a job you love. Maybe you make more money and that education, job, or money enables you to move to a better neighborhood, send your kids to a better school, pay for better medical care for a sick family member, or make a large donation to your favorite charity.

Again, that great leader made a difference in areas they didn't even know about.

You deserve a great leader. Stop tolerating bad leaders. Really. Fire them.

Before I get off this soapbox, let me say one more thing. I believe leadership is a skill. But I also believe People and Geeks are put into leadership roles who are not trained to be in that role. I believe those People or Geeks have a responsibility to seek out the leadership training they need to become the leaders that the people in their charge deserve.

If you are a leader and you are not serving your People and Geeks, you have a choice: Get Better or Step Down. Don't make People's life worse because you don't treat the job with the reverence that it deserves.

CONSEQUENCES OF INEXPERIENCED, INCOMPETENT, OR BAD LEADERS

There are myriad articles on the internet about the consequences of poor leaders. If you want to read more, use your favorite search engine and be prepared with a bottle of antidepressants.

Bad leaders cause poor financial performance, project failure, lower morale, lower productivity, higher employee turnover, higher employee death-rates, lower quality products, lower customer service scores, higher internal theft, higher internal malicious acts, higher legal claims, and earthquakes. That's right, I blame bad leaders for every earthquake. Ever. Prove me wrong.

End of rant.

Problem 3: Connecting the Dots (or Complexity Kills)

I was sitting in the board room of a Fortune 500 holding company around a large dark wood table fulling with people who made more in a year than I made in a lifetime. They had 9 major divisions each with their own operations, financials, and HR systems. Each division had shared information between the three major systems, but not between each other. Now the holding company wanted all the systems to sync to the holding company for consolidated reporting without adding any headcount.

"How hard can that be?" asked the CTO.

"Nearly impossible," I answered.

CTO scoffed, "We are only adding one new system: the reporting system. We are talking about 9 divisions supporting 3 systems. All they have to do is connect their systems to our system. How hard can that be?"

I answered, "Actually, you are creating a connection from each of the three division systems to the *ETL* service and another connection from the ETL service to the consolidated reporting. So that's six connections per division. My math says that's 54 connections."

ETL

Think translator. An ETL is like someone who speaks Japanese, French, Mandarin, and English. He can translate from Japanese to French or Japanese to Mandarin or Japanese to English or... You get it

I asked the IT Manager of one division, "How often do you make changes to one of your systems that break the sharing with the other two systems?"

"Every week," he said.

I turned back to the CTO. "Do you see the problem? It's not the number of systems. It's the number of connections to the systems? Your plan will break more often than it will be up."

People sometimes believe that the number of Geeks in an IT Department should be related to the number of things the Geeks support. In general, this is right, but the relationship isn't the way that people assume.

Think about Microsoft Office Suite. One of the things that makes Microsoft valuable is the connectedness between the applications. For example, I can make an Excel spreadsheet and embed the spreadsheet in a PowerPoint presentation. Then I can take the PowerPoint presentation and export it to Microsoft Word. I could take that Word document and turn it into an Outlook template for all new emails and I could then drag the email to my Outlook calendar to create a meeting appointment! Cool, huh?

Geeks often get asked to connect programs. Questions like, "Can you get SalesForce to talk to Microsoft Great Plains? Can you pull the information out of this spreadsheet into this database? Then can we get the punch-in/punch-out information from the time clocks into the payroll system? And then make them all talk to one another!" By connecting applications, it's easier for Business People to collaborate, faster for customers to send in orders, easier to get paid, or pay bills, etc, etc...

Geeks love to help People by connecting applications together to make the business more efficient. Geeks are helpful by nature. But each connection causes a geometric growth in complexity. Let me demonstrate.

Let's start with an oversimplified assumption. It takes one Geek to support something that is a "complexity 1". A "complexity 2" is two Geeks. "Complexity 3" is three Geeks. You get the idea. I don't think one Geek can only support one application. It's just an example.

Warning: Some light math ahead but stick with me. If you get this, it will blow your mind.

If a Geek supports one application, they only one support that one application. This hexagon represents a single application. That's a complexity 1. One Geek.

If the IT Department has two applications, you might think to support the two applications they need two Geeks. Very logical. But, if the applications are connected, to support the two applications plus the connection between the two applications, you need three Geeks, not two. Two connected applications have a total complexity of 3 (2 applications plus 1 connection). The two hexagons are applications. The line represents the connection between those two applications.

If the Geeks support three connected applications, they need to support those three applications, plus the connection between those three applications. This is a complexity of six (3 applications plus 3 connections). Six Geeks, not three.

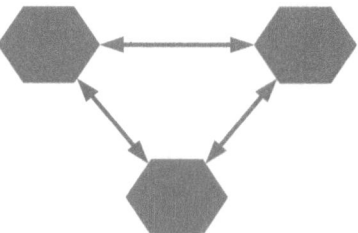

With four applications, things start to get interesting. You need ten Geeks to support four applications and six connections, or complexity of 10.

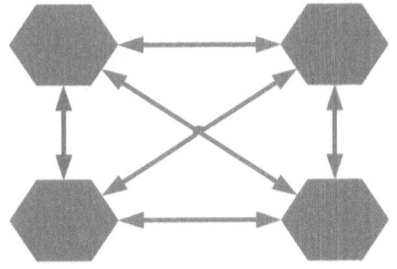

In fact, if we jump ahead a bit, you can see that eight applications get pretty crazy. Eight interconnected applications have 28 connections or complexity of 36 things to support.

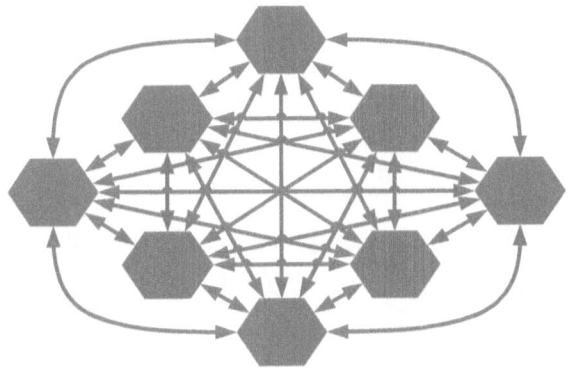

There is a relationship between connected/integrated applications and the number of Geeks, but that number isn't linear. It's geometric. The formula n(n+1)/2 can quickly calculate the total number of applications and connections where n is the number of applications. Resulting in a curve like this.

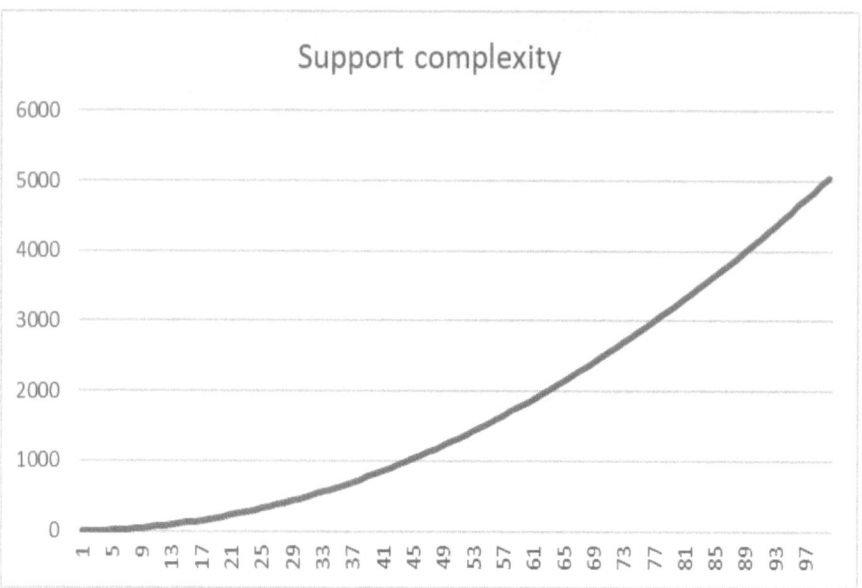

Support complexity

With 100 connected applications, the complexity is about the same as supporting 5,000 independent applications. With 500 connected applications in War Story 6, the complexity is about the same as 125,250 applications.

CONSEQUENCES OF COMPLEXITY

In a real-world sense, each extra connected application reduces the Geeks ability to deliver future value. **Geeks become so tied-up with maintaining the current complex system of interconnected applications that they don't have time to do anything but support the old complex system**. The Business People blame the Geeks for not delivering new features and programs they need. The Geeks blame the People for not giving them enough staff.

PROBLEM 3A: CONNECTING THE DOTS & COMMUNICATION OVERHEAD

Interestingly, this same dynamic applies to people communicating. Have you ever been in an email thread where someone replies to all, then someone else replies to all, then a third person replies to all to the first message _and_ to the second message? Then everything breaks loose, and you have no idea what anyone is saying? Same dots. Same complexity. Same math.

If communication between two people takes 1 minute, then communication between n people takes $n(n-1)/2$ minutes. If there's a 1% chance that someone will misunderstand something, with each person in the telephone game, the chance of miscommunication increases geometrically using the same formula. I call that **Communication Overhead**. That's why smaller meetings are more efficient. Less time spent talking to one another. Less chance of a misunderstanding. This is also one of the reasons that I love Wiio's Law: "Communication usually fails, except by accident."

Another problem the stories represent is a misunderstanding of expectations. War Story 3, 5, and 6 illustrate where the Geek thought they were doing their job, but they weren't. That misunderstanding caused the problems that challenged the Business People and the Geeks.

In War Story 3, the network security Geek thought his job was to **keep everything secure**, and the best way to keep everything secure was to make it nearly impossible to use. If something was usable, the Geek would only give it to the people who were worthy and no one could lift that Mjölnir. Not even Cap. We miss you, Steve.

In War Story 5, the Geeks thought their job was to keep the company's most precious asset: the **customer database safe**. If the data got corrupted, the nonprofit would have lost all its customer data, all of the transactions that they were legally required to maintain, and the nonprofit's reputation with all of their partners. The database was the organization to the Geeks. They were doing their job; they were protecting the company.

In War Story 6, the Geeks and CIO thought their job was to create computer applications that the company requested. To **create every application** that the company needed. The Geeks reasoned that Business People wouldn't request something that didn't add value, right? And that's what the Geeks did. Trapping themselves and the Business into a labyrinthine web of software. This ultimately resulted in being **unable to create valuable applications**. Jim Collins said, "Good is the enemy of great." That applies here. By creating an app for every good idea, the Geeks were unable to create the apps for the great ideas the company needed.

How can someone do what they think is right, but end up hurting their company, their department, and themselves? Because they thought they were doing what they were hired to do and no one had ever corrected them. The CEO in War Story 3 thought that when he requested remote access, the security Geek would understand that giving him access was the Geek's job. But the Geek thought he was being paid to secure the network and that the CEO didn't understand all the security risks. The Geek thought by saying "no" he was keeping the company safe and wasn't burdening the CEO with a Geek-Speak explanation of security. The Geek probably went home feeling great about saving the company from hackers and saving the CEO from the burdens of security. Good Geek.

CONSEQUENCES OF MISUNDERSTANDING THE EXPECTATIONS

By creating new applications in War Story 6, the CIO and Geeks were enabling the Business People and never had to say, "No, we can't create a new application for that". By saying "no," to everything the Geek in War Story 3 thought that he was helping keep the company safe. By controlling access in War Story 5, the Geeks thought that they were protecting the company's most valuable resource. No one would blame them for wanting to protect the company, right? Yet, shockingly, that's exactly what happened. Blame turned this Geek into the enemy.

Problem 5: My Precious

In War Story 1, 2, and 3, I told you about IT departments that hung on to old junk that no longer had value. They had closets full of old junk that should have been thrown out. But it goes much deeper than old pieces and parts, it might be old applications or old ideas too.

In War Story 1, the Business People hung on to an old application that ran the company for nearly a decade. That application had grown the company from a tiny little mom-and-pop company to a decent-sized business, employing hundreds and hundreds of People and Geeks. But they couldn't let it go. Whenever someone talked about replacing the application, the owners would say, "This system took us from a half-million-dollar company to a hundred-million-dollar company, why should we change now."

In War Story 3, the Geeks hung on to illogical fears about wireless, illogical hatred of Microsoft and Apple, and an ERP that was financially crippling the organization.

In War Story 4, the CEO hung on to an application that was hurting his employees and his customers and hung on to control that he no longer added value to the organization.

In War Story 5, the Geeks hung on to an application they built that was hurting the Business People and the customers.

In War Story 6, the CIO and Geeks hung on to an outdated idea that they had to write every application, rather than buy them.

Why do People like to keep junk that's not needed anymore? If you ask them, they will give you a dozen logical reasons. Some of which sound well-thought-out and completely rational on the surface. Geeks are especially adept at this because Geeks blind People with Geek-speak. They know you don't know if they actually need that junk, so they dazzle you with technological jargon until you walk away.

In reality, People and Geeks like to think they are logical, rational decision-makers. And history has proven this is a complete and totally wrong. I'll make my case, with a personal character flaw: I am fat.

Is being overweight bad for me? Yup. Do I know being overweight is bad for me? Yup. Did my doctor tell me last visit that being overweight is bad for me? Yup. Have I read 374,101 books on diets, exercise, and lifestyle changes telling me that being overweight is bad for me? Yup. Am I going to eat this entire box of chocolate frosted chocolate Pop-Tarts for breakfast while I type this chapter? You bet I am.

Do you think **more information** will change my behavior?

Example 2: I work with a guy who smokes. A lot. He smokes like I cuss. He smokes like it's his job. Do you think he knows smoking is bad for him? If I said, "Did you know smoking causes lung cancer?", would he would jump to his feet and say, "WOW! Really?" and change his life?

I hang with this guy during his smoke breaks. It was an opportunity to invest in his leadership development. I don't smoke at all. I try to stay upwind because cigarette smoke makes my allergies go nuts, but I wanted to hang with him and his smoke breaks are a less tense environment for deep conversations. During one smoke break, the guy said to me, "You're the only person who doesn't complain about smoking." I said, "You don't complain about overeating. I don't complain about smoking. If I ever get my act together, maybe we will talk." That's a Biblical principle, dealing with your own problems before worrying about everyone else's. I do call myself a Christian. But religion is another topic loaded with emotion.

The smoking-guy and I hoard habits that are not helpful. The Geeks and People in the War Stories hoard junk that is not helpful. **It's not logical. It's emotional.**

The more emotional people are the less logic helps. Have you ever been in an argument where the other person is super-emotional?

Losing their mind, screaming, tears, red-faced emotional? Do you win that argument by stating the facts? If you say 'yes', I'm going to call you a bold-faced liar.

The People and Geeks in the War Stories had an emotional connection with the junk in their lives. Even though the junk was causing them pain, hurting other people, and hurting their company, they couldn't let it go.

CONSEQUENCES OF HOARDING JUNK

Junk takes up space, time, and money. If you got rid of everything in your garage that you hadn't used in the last six months, I'll bet you could put your car in there. You might say, "But it's out of the way... in the garage." But when you need it, you have to look (at least) twice as long to find anything. And even if you argue that you are super-duper organized and you can find everything in 32 milliseconds, you are still paying for a section of your house just to store old junk.

But **my logical arguments are not going to convince you**, but this isn't a logical decision.

"Junk takes up space, time, and money" is true of the bits & bytes and pieces & parts of IT and, of business processes. You can easily detect those because someone will say, "We've always done it that way."

In Section 3, we address how to deal with emotional attachment.

PROBLEM 6: STAY IN YOUR LANE, BRO.

"Stay in your lane" means "Mind your own business" or "Bugger off, you cheeky scallywag! I'll have none of your barmy botch work!". It's one way to tell someone that you don't want to hear what they think about something that is not your responsibility. And that terrible attitude shuts down innovation pretty quick.

Technology can enable productivity for the Business People. Sometimes Geeks can do really cool things to make the business better but on the surface. These problems don't seem like Geek problems. Nothing's broken after all. You just want your Geeks to fix your computer and shut up. For example, the triplicate printer and vacuum tube system worked great, just the way it was.

I had just started with the company in War Story 1, probably not even two hours at my desk when I heard the raspy voice scream over the PA, "ORDER UP!!!"

"What was that?" I asked Tom, Dick, and Harry, the current Geeks.

They explained about the vacuum tube and getting orders out to the plant.

I asked how often that happened. They responded about a couple of times an hour. I asked, "Can't we configure the PA, so that the plant hears the announcement, but the office doesn't?"

Maybe? I don't know.

I continued, "Or even better. Let's set up a printer in the plant, so when an order comes in a copy just prints there too. No tearing triplicate paper. No screaming into a PA."

"But what will Phyllis do? That's her job," they asked.

"Something else that adds value," I said.

53

Re-engineering the order receiving process was not a tech problem, but sometimes Geeks don't speak up when they can help. Geeks might not feel like they should speak up, might not feel like the ideas are welcome, or might not know about options that could help.

That being said, technology is not always the answer.

A global manufacturer shipped its products in reusable shipping containers as part of an environmental improvement initiative. The customers liked the containers so much, they kept them to ship their own products in rather than return them. The VP of Operations asked me about implanting tracking tech in the containers because the containers cost $100 a unit and the company had been losing about 10 containers a week or over $50,000 a year.

I said, "Someone might make tech to do that, but why not just put a $100 refundable deposit on the customer invoice? If they keep the container, we can buy a new one. If they return it within 30 days, we take the $100 off their invoice. That's $0 tech cost and a phone call to finance to implement."

I've never felt the need to stay in my lane. If I have an idea about anything, I'll speak up. If it's a stupid idea, oh well, I've had a lot of those. If it's a good idea, if I stay in my lane, the company might miss an opportunity to improve.

COMPLAINING IS NOT HELPING.

This is not permission to go to your IT department sharing your observations about everything that is wrong. You aren't providing solutions. You are recounting the facts without helping. That's complaining.

Here's the difference. Imagine two of your friends have joined you at your house. The three of you are watching the game.

> Complaining Friend: "It's really hot in here. Super-hot. And what's that smell? Can't you fix that? Are you cooking something? Cause it smells like it's done. A while ago. And I think I'm allergic to whatever it is 'cause my eyes are burning and (cough, cough), it's hard to breathe."

> Helping Friend: "Dude, your house is on fire. Let's get out of here. I'll call 911."

Same situation. Who helped? Are you going to be the complaining friend or the helping friend?

CONSEQUENCES OF STAYING IN YOUR LANE.

Staying in your lane results in information silos. One group of people are the only ones who understand something. Those people hold all the cards. They are in control, which they think keeps their job safe. But it does not.

When Business People or Geeks "stay in their lane", they are not looking at the entire business and attempting to add value wherever they can. For the best companies, employee innovation and ownership are cornerstones of productivity. If your company doesn't actively encourage employees to step out of their lane, you are missing out. A fancy poster on the wall talking about the value of innovation isn't enough. Words are cheap.

Problem 7: The Wrong Investments

Some People see the IT Departments as a money pit. Like Tom Hanks and Shelley Long's house, the money goes in and nothing comes out. After the money's gone, IT shows up like Oliver Twist at the CFO's door, bowl outstretched, asking, "Please, sir. Can I have some more?"

This is not that. I'm not going to tell you to give the IT Department more money and all of your problems will go away. If you want all of your problems to go away, send your check to me at...

Just kidding.

The problem isn't more money. The problem is the money is spent on the wrong things.

When I was eight or nine, my grandparents gave me $100 for my birthday. That was a ton of money for me because we were dirt poor, my dad had died a couple of years earlier, and my mom was working to keep me clothed and feed. I know this now, but in my eight-year-old brain, I saw mountains and mountains of toys.

I talked someone into taking me to the toy store, lied and said my mom said I could buy whatever I wanted, and spent every last dime on cheap shiny plastic junk. Sorry, mom.

Sometimes IT budgets work like that. Not on toys. But on items that seem great in the moment, but from another angle, don't provide value to the business.

Remember, value is an important word. "Value" doesn't mean "important". Value is what customers will pay for. Value is what gets more business in the door, more dollars per sale, or more margin.

In War Story 3, the company had invested in an ERP which was way oversized for their company. An ERP can add a lot of value, but this was the top of the line, enterprise-grade ERP and the Geeks had signed a contract that gave them every add-on that the ERP sold. The ERP ended up costing about 1% of the company's gross sales. That's ridiculous.

Also, in War Story 3, the security Geek was spending money on security like he was protecting Area 51. Security is <u>necessary</u>, but it was not <u>valuable</u> to that company. If that company had the best security in the world, they wouldn't have sold one extra dollar of product or made one extra dollar in revenue.

In War Story 6, some of the Geeks had written applications that did not add value. For example, one Geek wrote some software that when someone started a new email, it added "Good morning", "Good afternoon", or "Good evening" to the beginning of the email based on the time of day. Neat, but didn't make the company one dollar.

THE CONSEQUENCES OF WRONG INVESTMENTS

When Geeks spend money and don't deliver value, the Business People stop giving them money. Period. Then they start cutting budgets. Then jobs. If you are a Geek and you say, "That's not fair!" It happens with every department. If a Sales department spends money but doesn't sell anything, the company cuts its budget.

Not at all coincidentally, because many Geeks have been through the IT cuts when the money goes away, they become hoarders (Problem 5). At some time in their past, the business started cutting funding and they had to keep things running with duct tape, baling wire, and the left-over scraps from their junk pile.

It's the circle of life....and it moves us all...

In War Story 4, I told you about a CEO that controlled every detail even down to where people sat. War Story 6 highlights some micromanagement behaviors by the CIO towards her staff. A while ago, I had an opportunity to talk to some individual contributors about their experience with micromanagement. The discussion was interesting. It wasn't a planned discussion. The topic of "micromanagement" came up spontaneously while I was sitting in a team meeting. All the Geeks agreed micromanagement was bad and that they hated being micromanaged. So I asked, "How do you define micromanagement?"

Everyone could talk about times they felt had micromanaged, but found it challenging to nail down a clear definition. However, the stories are insightful.

One Geek told a story about a manager telling him to do a task. The Geek asked, "why?" because thought there might be a better solution. The manager said, "You don't need to know why. Just do what I told you."

Another Geek told another story about a manager telling him how to do a task. When the Geek found another, more efficient way to complete the work, the manager became hostile and insisted he does the task the original way. The Geek later found out the manager had created the original methodology.

A different Geek needed time to implement a solution. He told his boss that it would take him a week to "do it right." His boss told him that he needed it now and he needed to do it faster.

Yet another Geek told a story about her manager asking her for daily updates on a project that would take months to complete and that did not change daily. When she asked about the frequency of the updates, her manager told her that she needed to continue the daily updates.

A common misconception is that high-pressure environments, with hard deadlines and demanding work, causes people to feel micromanaged. But the Geeks said the most fun they ever had was in high-pressure situations. High-pressure did not make them feel micromanaged because they were confident that they could work hard and get things done. However, they also said that an insecure manager is more likely to micromanage people during high-pressure situations. The manager's insecurity makes them feel like they must give specific directions, push people to go faster and faster, and demand frequent updates.

CONSEQUENCES OF MICROMANAGEMENT

Micromanagement fundamentally is a trust issue. The victim feels untrusted, disrespected, and devalued. Those being micromanaged said the manager needs to be in control because they felt threatened by someone else or insecure. The micromanager does not trust his staff member's skills, time estimates, knowledge, or communication.

Sometimes things are so broken that no one has time to breathe, to think, or to plan for anything that getting through today. You are so busy that you can't remember if you took lunch, and you have to look at your phone to remember what day of the week it is. Maybe all the complexity has finally caught up with your Geeks and now they simply can't do anything else but keep the stuff running. Maybe the lack of delivering value has cut the IT budget to the bone and the Geeks are just trying to keep the email up.

That's firefighting-mode and it's dangerous for a couple of reasons. The first reason is that you don't have time to do the right thing. The second reason firefighting-mode is dangerous: you can learn to like it. Some people call this firefighter's syndrome. It's really toxic.

In War Story 4, the Geeks were flooded with 15,000 (really) emails a day from automated systems saying "Help! This is broken" or "Help! That is broken!" To read 15,000 emails a day, you need to read an email every 5.8 seconds 24 hours a day 7 days a week. The IT Director liked it because he felt important. "Look how busy I am!" he would say. He hid in his office sorting emails and counting emails but never fixing the problems causing the emails. If the Geeks fixed all the problems, what would he do? The Geeks complained about all the work, but everyone admired them. As they scurried past the Geeks' cubicles, the Business People would whisper in awe, "Leave them alone. Did you hear they get 15,000 emails a day!"

No one thanks a firefighter for preventing fires. No business Person has ever said to a Geek, "Dude! Everything worked perfectly today again! I connected my computer to another computer halfway around the world and downloaded the equivalent of 3,000 novels in under an hour. It worked flawlessly. Thanks, man!" (This is what your computer does when you stream an HD video for an hour. Technology is pretty awe-inspiring when you understand it.) But if something breaks and a business Person can't connect to that same webinar and the Geek fixes the problem quickly, the Geek will often hear, "Thanks for helping me so fast today! You really did great!"

That little bit of endorphins from that gratitude... it's like crack for Humans. That's how you train firefighting syndrome.

In War Story 6, we see an IT Department in full firefighting mode. The complexity and wrong investments resulted in a team unable to do anything except deal with the most urgent fires. It hadn't devolved into firefighting syndrome; the Geeks wanted to help but they felt helpless. The CIO couldn't dig them out of the hole she had made and needed someone to blame. She was too weak of a leader to see her part in the problem and so she blamed the team. If they worked harder, this would all go away.

CONSEQUENCES OF BEING TOO BUSY TO DO THE RIGHT THINGS

Being in firefighting-mode results in demoralized Geeks or, worse, toxic firefighter-syndrome. It results in the technology problems perpetuating, which in turn leads to finger-pointing, blames, them vs us toxic cultures.

CHAPTER 4: PROBLEMS ASSEMBLE!

Wouldn't it be nice if these were ten independent problems? I could give you a nice little checklist so that you could highlight the problems that you think you are experiencing, look up the solutions, and *poof* everything is better. The magical British nanny floats away on her umbrella, the hoodlum gets the prom queen, Daniel-san lands that completely ineffective kick... credits roll... happily ever after...

Unfortunately, each of these problems feeds the other in a linked group of interdependent things... like a cluster of broken things... if only there was a single catchy word that would summarize a situation like that...

CLUSTER-BROKEN

Unfortunately, under-skilled Geeks lead to wrong investments, complexity, firefighting, micromanagement, blame, silos, unclear expectations, and hoarding. Wrong investments lead to complexity, firefighting, micromanagement, blame, silos, unclear expectations, hoarding, under-skilled leaders, and under-skilled Geeks. Complexity lead to firefighting, micromanagement, blame, silos, unclear expectations, hoarding, and wrong investments. Firefighting leads to complexity, micromanagement, blame, silos, unclear expectations, hoarding, under-skilled leaders, wrong investments, and under-skilled Geeks. Micromanagement leads to blame, silos, hoarding, under-skilled leaders, wrong investments, firefighting, and under-skilled Geeks. Blame leads to micromanagement, silos, hoarding, under-skilled leaders, wrong investments, firefighting, and under-skilled Geeks. Under skilled leaders lead to complexity, micromanagement, blame, silos, unclear expectations, hoarding, wrong investments, firefighting, and under-skilled Geeks. Silos lead to complexity, micromanagement, blame, unclear expectations, hoarding, under-skilled leaders, wrong investments, firefighting, and under-skilled Geeks. Hoarding leads to complexity, micromanagement, silos, unclear expectations, under-skilled leaders, wrong investments, firefighting, under-skilled Geeks, and dragons which come to take all your dwarven gold.

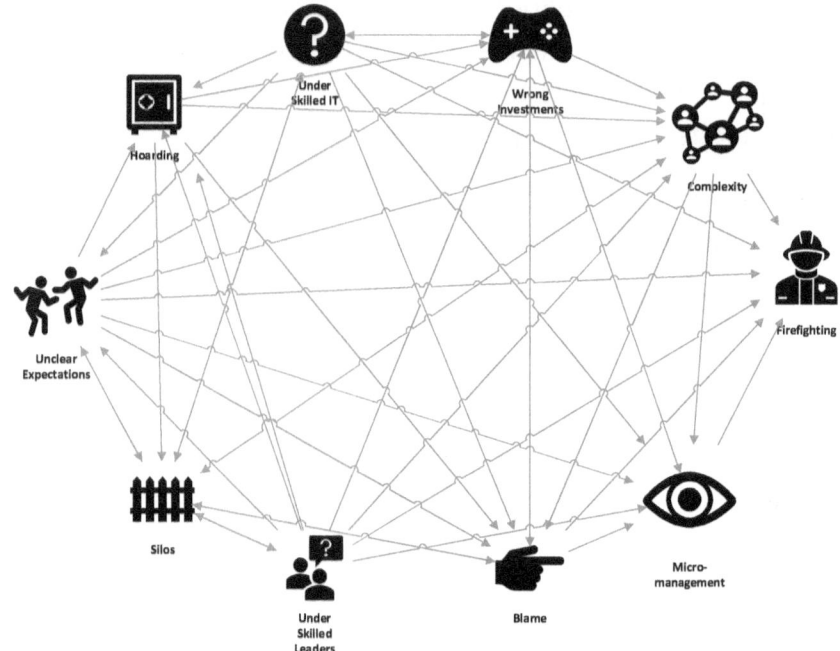

In this case, a picture is worth 138 words.

If you feel like Rusty when Clark gave him the giant knot of Christmas lights, you should. If you think a complex problem has a simple solution, your wrong. No silver bullets.

Time to untie this Gordian's knot of misery.

SECTION 3: FIX IT

CHAPTER 5: WHAT IS FIXED IT?

Fixed IT contributes to the value creation of your company. That means IT increases sales or increases profit. One way or another fixed IT makes your company money. The activities that consume the most time and money create the most value. The Geeks on an fixed IT department have the training and skills to support value creation. They understand the value proposition and competencies of the company. Because they understand, the value proposition and competencies, the Geeks come up with useful suggestions to increase value.

How does that sound? Like a dream? It can happen. You can make it happen. But…

Remember when I told you that there were no silver bullets. **Remember** when I told you that if we don't work together, this situation is never going to get better?

Now's the time you're going to put your money where your mouth is.

If you think that you can just change one thing and have everything get better, you've completely missed the entire point.

Are you really committed to doing what it takes to fix your IT?

Because we need to start from the ground up to fix IT.

Have you ever peeled an onion and found a brown spot, so you peel off another layer and the brown spot gets bigger, so you peel off another layer and another layer and the brown spot gets bigger and bigger until you realized that the entire onion is rotten? That's what broken IT is. An onion rotted to the core.

You cannot peel off a layer and fix this. The problem isn't a person or a department or a process. It's the entire onion. I'm going to challenge your entire business's approach to IT.

> "Ogres are like onions... Onions
> have layers. Ogres have layers.
> Onions have layers. You get it? We
> both have layers."
>
> Shrek from *Shrek.*

I'm going to give you an entirely--new onion.

CHAPTER 6: BUILDING A FOUNDATION

IT is part of your business. Period. They are not some separate thing that exists in a magical universe where fundamental business principles do not exist (although sometimes we Geeks wish we did or may act as if we do.) We need to rethink IT to do what it should do: Add Value to The Business.

Remember the definition of value from earlier:

> Value [/ˈvalyo͞o/]
>
> *Noun*
>
> 1. Anything your customer will pay for.
> 2. That's it. Sorry, buddy.

It's also important to remember IT should add value to the <u>business</u>. Not a department. Not someone's pet project. Not to IT. And the business of your business is...

Why Your Business Exists: Value

Customers buy your stuff. Whether your stuff is a thing, a service, or an idea, you have customers and they buy your stuff.

- If you make soap (a thing), your customers buy your soap because it has "something" that they want more than another soap. They give you money to have that "something"
- If you wash dogs (a service), your customers choose you to wash their dog because you have "something" that they want more than another dog washer. It could be a relationship with the dog, a friendly smile, or you are the closest... but it is "something". They give you money for that something.

- If you run a nonprofit charity that raises money for saving the Kitti's hog-nosed bat (an idea), your donors and volunteers are your customers (they give you something of value: money or time) for "something" that your charity does. It could be a shared belief about how cute Kitti's hog-nosed bat is, it could be community service to avoid jail, it could be part of a corporate social responsibility initiative and part of their "we are not an evil empire" media campaign. The point is: you provide something that they value in exchange for something you value.

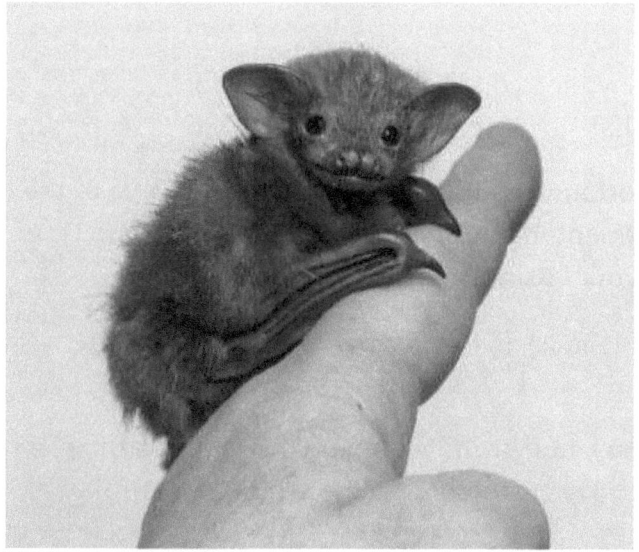

Seriously, look how cute it is.

These "somethings" are how your business generates value or your Customer-Value-Proposition (CVP).

Your business can generate value through a variety of Customer-Value-Propositions (CVP), such as features/benefits/attributes, price, availability/exclusivity, quality, brand awareness/reputation, variety, service, relationship, convenience, customization/personalization, or association with another value (such as environmental products or products designed to appeal to a specific race, nationality, religious group).

Knowing how your business's Customer-Value-Proposition (CVP) is very important for this book. Actually, it's important for running a business.

Competitors in the same business have different CVPs. For example, let's create three imaginary coffee shops.

Five-Pointed-Deer is a nationally-recognized, trendy coffee shop that sells coffee and a variety of sugary desserts disguised as coffee drinks. The customers come there because they have good coffee (features), they are everywhere (availability), they are consistent (quality), they advertise a lot (brand awareness), the service is good (duh - service), and they make every sugary drink under the sun (variety) and if they don't they'll mix up whatever concoction you can imagine.

Your-Neighborhood-Coffee-Shop is a local, small-town coffee shop that tries to position itself as the anti-Five-Pointed-Deer. The customers come there because they have coffee from a local roaster (features), they learn all the regulars' names and drink preferences (relationships), and association with their small town by supporting other small-town events.

I-Guess-This-Is-Coffee is a coffee shop started by a couple of retired buddies as a place to get together and hang out. They didn't want a bunch of kids or that-crap-kids-are-calling-music-now-a-days playing. They wanted someplace to talk with their friends and get a cup of joe. Some other retirees started coming and it's become the place-to-be for the local silver-haired people. The coffee is whatever's-cheapest-at-the-grocery-this-week, run through a drip coffee maker that looks older than the two guys running the place, and served in some Styrofoam cups. Get it yourself and put a buck in the jar. People come there for the price (cheap), the relationships (everybody knows everybody), and the association with retirees.

All three fictional places sell coffee but understanding their CVPs makes a world of difference. It makes a difference in how the coffee shops market, how they operate, and it should make a difference in how they approach IT.

Take a few minutes to fill this out:

My business creates value for our customers by: _____

_____

_____

_____

Now, you might be thinking that this has nothing to do with IT. **That's the problem**. That's why IT is broken (both meanings).

Allow me to sing you a song using my best John Lennon impression: "Imagine all the departments…Generating CVP (ah ah ah)"

Seriously, imagine an IT department where the money into IT generated value for the customer, which generated profit for the business. Imagine every time you gave IT $100,000, sales (top line) increased $200,00, or operating costs dropped $200,000. You now get a 200% return on every dollar you put in. How much money would you put in IT? I'd give them every dollar I could. IT would be like a money-printing machine.

I'm <u>not</u> saying you can get your IT Department to a 200% return. I'm not saying that IT will only do things that customers will pay for. No department does this. Do you think the customer cares about whether or not you have a copier in HR? Or an executive assistant? Or plants in the office? **I am saying if we align IT with your business's CVP, we can get a <u>better</u> return.** Are we on the same page again? Good.

CHAPTER 7: HOW YOU DO WHAT YOU DO

You wrote down your Customer-Value-Propositions (CVP) in the last chapter, right? No? I thought you wanted to fix IT? Go back. Do it now.

Seriously. Turn back two pages.

I can wait here all day...

There. Don't you feel better?

The next step is to figure out how you do the things that create the value. What are you good at that enables your company to provide great service or make the highest quality thing-a-mabobs or establish exclusive partnerships with the Alien Overlords of Planet X… however you defined value before. The things that you do that create value are your business's competencies or Value-Supporting-Competencies (VSC). Value-Supporting-Competencies (VSC) are the engines that produce value.

Let's revisit one of the fictional coffee shops:

Five-Pointed-Deer value propositions:

- Good coffee (features)
- Located everywhere (availability)
- Consistent (quality)
- Advertising (brand awareness)
- Good service
- Lots of different sugary drinks
- Customized sugary drinks

To determine the Value-Supporting-Competencies (VSC) that enable creating value, Five-Pointed-Deer must ask, "How do we do _____?" for each value-proposition.

- **How does Five-Pointed-Deer get good coffee?** They use their size to negotiate exclusive supplier agreements with the best bean suppliers. They taste test everything. They only ship the best beans to their ubiquitous caffeine & sugar crack houses.
- **How does Five-Pointed-Deer establish locations everywhere?** Profitable growth and reinvesting cash in new store acquisition.
- **How does Five-Pointed-Deer ensure consistency?** They taste test everything. They only ship the best beans to their coffee shops.

74

- **How does Five-Pointed-Deer create brand awareness?** Dedicated budget to advertising and social media presence.
- **How does Five-Pointed-Deer provide good service?** Standardized extensive corporate training upon being hired and every six-months. Customer service is reinforced in every meeting and message from the home office. And the shock collars hidden in the workers' uniforms.
- **How does Five-Pointed-Deer have so many different sugary drinks?** All custom orders from all locations are sent back to the corporate office. For repeated orders for the same custom drink, a test kitchen reproduces the recipe. We test consumer response and if it's positive, we add it to the menu, usually as a limited-time drink.
- **How does Five-Pointed-Deer customize sugary drinks?** By maintaining a large variety of flavored sugar goop to pour in coffee and making customers aware that they can have it however they like.

Based on that analysis, we could say Five-Pointed-Deer's competencies are:

- Exclusive supplier agreements with bean suppliers
- Taste-testing facilities
- Reinvesting profits in new store acquisition
- Advertising and social media
- Corporate training and retraining (and shock collars)
- Analyzing store sales to identify new concoctions
- Keeping stores stocked with lots of flavors

Let's do one more just to make sure we've got it.

Your-Neighborhood-Coffee-Shop value propositions:

- Coffee from a local roaster
- Learn all the regulars' names and drink preferences

- Association with their small town by supporting other small-town events.

Now, let's figure out their Value-Supporting-Competencies (VSC):

- **How does Your-Neighborhood-Coffee-Shop get coffee from a local roaster?** They found a local roaster online and visited them. They talked to the local roaster about the challenges of being a local business and offered to work together.
- **How does Your-Neighborhood-Coffee-Shop learn all the regulars' names?** They tell employees to ask the customers' name and use it three times when they first meet. They put the customers' name with the order into their computer. They have weekly contests with decent prizes for the employee who gets the most names right and orders right.
- **How does Your-Neighborhood-Coffee-Shop connect with their small town and support local events?** They monitor the local paper. If any new events appear, they visit the event coordinator and talk about the importance of supporting local events and local businesses and look for a way to work together.

Based on that analysis, we would say Your-Neighborhood-Coffee-Shop's VSC are:

- Connecting with local roasters
- Training employees on their values
- Connecting with local events.

Now, let's do your company. What does your company do to creates those values that customers pay for?

- How does your company do _____?

- How does your company do _____?

- How does your company do _____?

- How does your company do _____?

- How does your company do _____?

Now, turn that list into Value-Supporting-Competencies (VSC) (your company will probably have more than four):

1. _____

2. _____

3. _____

4. _____

You didn't think this book was going to give you a silver bullet, cookie-cutter solution, did you? Stop your whining and do the work.

CHAPTER 8: WHY WE DID ALL THAT

You might be wondering why we did that exercise.

Imagine you are the CEO of Five-Pointed-Deer Coffee. Remember, the things you do that make your company money (VSC) are:

- Exclusive supplier agreements with bean suppliers
- Taste-testing facilities
- Reinvesting profits in new store acquisition
- Advertising and social media
- Corporate training and retraining (and shock collars)
- Analyzing store sales to identify new concoctions
- Keeping stores stocked with lots of flavors

Imagine I'm your IT Director. Imagine Brad Pitt. Now think of the exact opposite of Brad Pitt. That's me.

I come to you and say, "I found a new business intelligence tool that can automatically analyze the store sales to identify repeat orders and identify new concoctions."

Are you interested?

Of course, you are.

What if I came to you and said, "I found a new business intelligence tool that can automatically find local coffee roasters and bring them to your attention."

Are you interested?

Of course not. You'd probably look at me, shake your head, and say, "David, you just don't understand the business."

I would leave, choking back the tears. You didn't need to be quite that mean.

Imagine you are the owner of Your-Neighborhood-Coffee-Shop. Me again. Opposite of Brad Pitt, but I've put on another 10 pounds after my emotionally crippling run-in with the CEO of Five-Pointed-Deer and shame eating 3-gallons of Ben & Jerry's Chubby Hubby (the irony!).

I say, "I can add a webcam to the cash registers so we can add our customers' pictures to their receipt with the customers' permission. We could use that learn our customers' names and faces even better."

Interested?

Absolutely.

Imagine instead I say, "I found a program online that will let us do automatic coffee bean orders with a global coffee roaster network! We can offer exotic coffees from around the world!"

Interested?

No. The second your local roaster finds out that you are offering the same coffee as every other coffee shop in that network, you will lose all credibility with him and maybe everyone else. People will think you've gone corporate.

If I was you, I would probably be thinking, "Your big reveal is the IT Department needs to bring us valuable ideas? Forget you and forget this book."

Nope.

That's not quite it. We aren't going to spend any new money on new ideas yet. We are going to use your competencies to decide what to do with your current IT initiatives.

CHAPTER 9: EVALUATING YOUR CURRENT IT (BUSINESS PERSON'S VERSION)

Your Geeks are doing something. Right now. This minute. While you're reading this book. Over 90% of C-level business leaders say that they have no idea what their IT Department does. Do you know what your IT Department is doing?

Should you?

Here's how to find out.

STEP 1: TALK TO A GEEK

Remember that most Geeks and Business People live in a state of near-cold-war. Most Geeks don't trust Business People. Geeks think they only come with unreasonable demands or complaints and have no desire to understand technology. Most Business People don't trust Geeks. They constantly need money, they seldom deliver value, are usually late, and Geeks have no desire to understand business.

And I'm telling you to break the détente. Make a Geek friend. You need at least one. To prove you aren't racist against Geeks.

Now that conversation can go a couple of ways:

> Business Person says, "Hey Geek, tell me everything your department does."

> Geek hears, "Hey Geek, justify your existence."

Or...

> Business Person says, "Hey Geek, I've been reading this cool book about how I can work better with IT. If I got you a copy, would you read it and see if it makes sense."

Geek hears, "Hey Geek, I'm trying to learn something. I value your opinion. Will you help me?"

Which of these conversations will go better?

STEP 2: GET A LIST OF THE CURRENT IT INITIATIVES.

At the start of this chapter, I suggested that your Geeks are doing something. The something might be building something new, fixing something old, or keeping something old working. Most of their activities are related to these three somethings.

A lot of Business People assume that "keeping something old working" isn't "that hard", but most IT Departments report that 80% of their time and budget going to this. In Geeks parlance, they talk about *KTLO (Keeping the Lights On)*. KTLO activities are generally mindless, soul-crushing activities that no Geek would willingly do, but if they don't do it, People will be pounding on their door with torches and pitchforks screaming, "WHY IS THE EMAIL DOWN AGAIN?!"

KTLO

Daily routine activities that Geeks need to do to keep your internet on, your email up, your computer free from viruses, your phone working, etc...

Ask your new Geek friend what the IT Department does in these three categories and make a list. Four items is an example. Your list size might vary.

Building Something New	Fixing Something Old	Keeping Something Working
1.	1.	1.
2.	2.	2.

| 3. | 3. | 3. |
| 4. | 4. | 4. |

Don't ask for how much time or the budget for each item. Depending on your Business Person – Geek cultural, it could be seen as an attempt to micromanage, which we have established is bad.

If you need a cost or time later, you can get it later. Right now, you are building a friendship with a Geek and understanding the world they live in.

If there is any Geek-speak in the list, admit ignorance and ask questions. Ignorance isn't bad. I'm ignorant about a lot of things: international tax laws, the entire Kardashian cult, how to give a colonoscopy, the names of any K-Pop Singers, how my wife makes such amazing oatmeal cookies, etc... Ignorance is only bad if you need to know something and your ego won't let you admit ignorance -or- if you pretend to know something about something that you are ignorant about.

Start with, "Hey Geek, you know I'm not an IT guy. Can you explain this to me so I non-Technical guy can understand? What's an Exchange server?" Or "What's a Server?"

Revise the list so that the Geek-speak is gone. Add anything new that comes up during your time talking to your new friend. If you have time, you might want to do this with a couple of Geeks. Geeks, like regular humans, are not perfect. One Geek may remember something that another Geek does not.

STEP 3: CATEGORIZE THE LIST

Once you feel like your investigation has produced a comprehensive list, we are going to connect competencies to activities.

	Building Something New	Keeping Something Old Working	Fixing Something Old
Strongly Tied to Competency	1. 2. 3. 4.	1. 2. 3. 4.	1. 2. 3. 4.
Might be Tied to Competency	1. 2. 3. 4.	1. 2. 3. 4.	1. 2. 3. 4.
No Relationship to Competency	1. 2. 3. 4.	1. 2. 3. 4.	1. 2. 3. 4.

To keep ourselves honest, put the number of the competency next to the IT Activity. Remember, just because something is in the "not related to a competency", does not mean we don't need to do it. It doesn't mean it's not important. For example, employee toilets don't add customer-value to a car manufacturer, but we still need toilets for the employees.

The most important thing is honesty and a critical eye.

You now have a nine-section matrix with nine different types of activities.

	Building Something New	Keeping Something Old Working	Fixing Something Old Broken
Strongly Tied to Competency	Type 1	Type 2	Type 3
Might be Tied to Competency	Type 4	Type 5	Type 6
No Relationship to Competency	Type 7	Type 8	Type 9

- Type 1 is building something new that is strongly tied to a competency.
- Type 2 is keeping something working that is strongly tied to a competency.
- Type 3 is fixing something old that is strongly tied to a competency.
- Type 4 is building something new that might be tied to a competency.
- Type 5 is keeping something working that might be tied to a competency.
- Type 6 is fixing something old that might be tied to a competency.
- Type 7 is building something new that is not tied to a competency.
- Type 8 is keeping something working that is not tied to a competency.
- Type 9 is fixing something old that is not tied to a competency.

> "We choose to innovate to add value. We choose to add value
> and innovate and do the other things, not because they are
> easy, but because they are hard, because that goal will serve the
> customer and measure the best of our IT competencies,
> because that challenge is one that we are willing to accept, one
> we are unwilling to postpone, and one which we intend to win."

David Rettig,
A completely original quote
Not at all paraphrased from JFK.
For reals.

STEP 4: ASSESS

You are now going to go through your current IT initiatives to ruthlessly assess each initiative, based on the activity type. In the Fix IT Framework, this is called Classify & Assess (C&A).

TYPE 1: SPACE RACE

This is Geeks creating something new that improves your organization's ability to deliver value. Invest in this with time and money. You want IT Departments doing this.

In a tactical sense, Space Race activities should not have too many fences. Do it and do it fast. **If the Geeks need to build something custom or customize an out of the box application, absolutely do it. Space Race activities will pay for themselves.**

TYPE 2: GOLDEN-EGG LAYING GOOSE

Feed the goose. **Golden-Egg Laying Goose activities enable your competencies and empower your company to make more money.** Hooah! That's exactly what you want. Massage that goose like it's a million-dollar Kobe steer. Sing it love songs. Buy it flowers. Tell it you love it every day.

In a tactical sense, look for ways to improve these activities. Again, Geeks should be free to customize these to improve value delivery.

TYPE 3: CONSTIPATED GOOSE

Somebody get that Goose a laxative. You had something working, delivering value, and it stopped. Type 4-9 activities need to be paused (at least) to give your Geeks more time to get this working again.

TYPE 4: WHEEL

<u>**Don't**</u> **reinvent** <u>**the wheel**</u>**!** If you aren't 100% positive this activity adds value, don't stop it; Buy it and use it out of the box. I don't care if it doesn't do everything you need. Don't customize it and don't develop it in-house.

Technology is a tool. Do you go to the hardware store and ask them to make you a pink hammer with a special grip because you like pink and a standard hammer gave you a blister once? No? Do you need a toaster that automatically butters your toaster when it's done? No? Stop thinking of Information Technology as anything other than a standard tool, just because you can.

Yes... yes... it would be super cool if you email automatically dumped to a PDF for storage on your file server and then texted you a GIF of a dancing cat, but you don't <u>need</u> it. It would be super cool if accounts payables hand-wrapped invoices in gift wrap – but that doesn't add value.

Stop preventing value-added activities chasing something that makes your life a little easier or seems neat-o but doesn't add customer value. If your customer wouldn't pay for it, you wasting your company's resource with pet projects. **Stop investing in activities that don't strongly link to value.**

In War Story 6, the IT Department had written time tracking apps. If this company had the best time tracking app in the world, would they sell one more thing-a-mabob? <u>No</u>. Stop wasting a limited resource, your company's Geeks' time, on non-value-add projects like this. Buy a standard hammer and do not customize it.

<u>Don't reinvent the wheel!</u>

TYPE 5: KEEP AIR IN THE TIRES

You didn't re-invent the wheel, right? You are just keeping the air in the tires. Do it. Do the minimum maintenance to keep the tires on the bus.

TYPE 6: FLAT TIRE

If you have an opportunity to replace some custom unicorn, snowflake custom wheel that the IT Department built with a standard wheel, do it now. Otherwise, fix the tire.

TYPE 7: ALIEN INVADER

Any new IT initiative that does not deliver customer-value to the organization needs to be killed. Mercilessly. With fire. Now. It doesn't matter if it's the CEO's pet project or if IT says, "99% complete...it will be ready tomorrow." Kill it. Dead. Nuke it from orbit. It's the only way to be sure.

Any Alien Invader project that you allow to complete will become a Mooch, where most IT departments spend 80% of your company's resources, draining your company's resources. You already have too many Melmacians in your house, drinking all your beer. You do not need more of that.

TYPE 8: THE MOOCH

Any existing IT initiative that does not add to delivering customer-value through a competency should be allowed to live, peacefully. Although it's a drain on the company's resources, someone likes The Mooch or it wouldn't still be around.

TYPE 9: MOOCH ON LIFE SUPPORT

Any IT effort spent on keeping the life support on is time and money thrown down the money-pit. IT is bringing something back to life only to make it a Mooch again. Let the Mooch rest-in-peace. Have a wake. Bring tequila. Invite me.

CHAPTER 9: EVALUATING YOUR CURRENT IT (GEEK'S VERSION)

Your Business People are doing something. Right now. This minute. While you're reading this book. Over 90% of Geeks say that they have no idea how their company makes money does. Do you know how your company makes money?

Should you?

Here's how to find out.

STEP `: MAKE A LIST OF THE CURRENT IT INITIATIVES.

We Geeks are generally busy building something new, fixing something old, or keeping something old working. Most of our activities are related to these three somethings.

Most IT Departments report that 80% of their time and budget going to "keeping something old working" or *KTLO (Keeping the Lights On)*. KTLO activities are generally mindless, soul-crushing activities that no Geek would willingly do, but if we don't do it, Business People will be pounding on their door with torches and pitchforks screaming, "WHY IS THE EMAIL DOWN AGAIN?!"

Break the list down like this:

Building Something New	Fixing Something Old	Keeping Something Working
1.	1.	1.
2.	2.	2.
3.	3.	3.
4.	4.	4.
5.	5.	5.
6.	6.	6.

Step 2: Talk to a Business Person

Remember that most Geeks and Business People live in a state of near-cold-war. Most Geeks don't trust Business People. Business People only come with unreasonable demands or complaints and have no desire to understand technology. Most Business People don't trust Geeks. They think we constantly need money, we seldom deliver value, are usually late, and Geeks have no desire to understand business. But we are going to shatter that myth.

You will break the détente. Make a Business Person friend. You need at least one. To prove you aren't racist against Business People. Pick someone in the organization with some influence, like a department manager, director, or C-level person, you'll see why in Chapter 11.

I would say something like this:

> Geek says, "Hey Business Person, I've been reading this cool book about how to deliver more value to the business. I really need some Business People support to make the changes we need in IT. Would you read it to any help me make the changes we need?"

> Business Person hears, "I realize that we aren't giving you the value you deserve. I'm sorry. I want to do better. Will you help me?"

Generally, Business People are a good lot. They are busy and get frustrated when stuff doesn't work. If you ask for help, they are generally decent human beings. Really. Try it.

You are going to need a Business Person. Try the words, "Executive Sponsor". That's someone who will help you overcome any internal resistance.

It's important that your Business Person friend reads this book prior to this next part, because "value" means different things to different Business People. Really. Also, some Business People don't really think about the relationship between Customer-Value-Propositions (CVP) and Value-Supporting-Competencies (VSC). Really really.

To some Business People, "value" can mean a principle or moral or code of behavior. Like those posters that hang on the walls, generally around HR's offices, saying "Teamwork" or "Integrity".

To some Business People, "value" can mean important. If you ask if it is "valuable", they might hear, "Is this project really important?" and think, "Who is this Geek to challenge my request?" then they will slap you across the cheek with a leather glove and challenge you to a sword fight to the death at dawn.

To some Business People, to this author, and to you, "value" means what the customer will pay for. We want them to mean CVP. If you don't get them to read this book, find another Business Person because this one is not committed to helping you.

STEP 3: CATEGORIZES THE LIST

Once you've found you a Business Person friend who speaks the same language as you, ask them to help you align your projects with VSC that support the company's Customer-Value-Propositions.

	Building Something New	Keeping Something Old Working	Fixing Something Old
Strongly Tied to Competency	1. 2. 3. 4.	1. 2. 3. 4.	1. 2. 3. 4.

Might be Tied to Competency	1. 2. 3. 4.	1. 2. 3. 4.	1. 2. 3. 4.
No Relationship to Competency	1. 2. 3. 4.	1. 2. 3. 4.	1. 2. 3. 4.

To keep ourselves honest, put the number of the competency next to the IT Activity. Remember, just because something is in the "not related to a competency", does not mean we don't need to do it. It doesn't mean it's not important. For example, employee toilets don't add customer-value to a car manufacturer, but we still need toilets for the employees.

The most important thing is honesty and a critical eye.

You now have a nine-section matrix with nine different types of IT projects.

	Building Something New	Keeping Something Old Working	Fixing Something Old Broken
Strongly Tied to Competency	Type 1	Type 2	Type 3
Might be Tied to Competency	Type 4	Type 5	Type 6
No Relationship to Competency	Type 7	Type 8	Type 9

- Type 1 is building something new that is strongly tied to a competency.

- Type 2 is keeping something working that is strongly tied to a competency.
- Type 3 is fixing something old that is strongly tied to a competency.
- Type 4 is building something new that might be tied to a competency.
- Type 5 is keeping something working that might be tied to a competency.
- Type 6 is fixing something old that might be tied to a competency.
- Type 7 is building something new that is not tied to a competency.
- Type 8 is keeping something working that is not tied to a competency.
- Type 9 is fixing something old that is not tied to a competency.

Step 4: Prioritize

You are now going to go through your current IT initiatives to ruthlessly cut out the fat, based on the activity type. In the Fix IT Framework, we call this Classify & Assess (C&A).

TYPE 1: SPACE RACE

We are creating something new that improves your organization's ability to deliver value. Invest in this with time and money. We want IT Departments doing this.

In a tactical sense, Space Race activities should not have too many fences. Do it and do it fast. **If this requires us to build something custom, or customize an out of the box application, absolutely do it. Space Race activities will pay for themselves.**

> "We choose to innovate to add value. We choose to add value
> and innovate and do the other things, not because they are
> easy, but because they are hard, because that goal will serve the
> customer and measure the best of our IT competencies,
> because that challenge is one that we are willing to accept, one
> we are unwilling to postpone, and one which we intend to win."

David Rettig,
A completely original quote
Not at all paraphrased from JFK.
See the previous chapter if you don't believe me.

TYPE 2: GOLDEN-EGG LAYING GOOSE

Feed the goose. **Golden-Egg Laying Goose activities enable your competencies and empower your company to make more money.** Hooah! That's exactly what you want. Massage that goose like it's a million-dollar Kobe steer. Sing it love songs. Buy it flowers. Tell it you love it every day.

In a tactical sense, look for ways to improve these activities. Again, Geeks should be free to customize these to improve value delivery.

TYPE 3: CONSTIPATED GOOSE

Somebody get that Goose a laxative. The business had something working, delivering value, and it stopped. Call a War Room and get that system back up.

TYPE 4: WHEEL

Don't reinvent the wheel! If you aren't 100% positive this activity adds value, don't stop it; Buy it and use it out of the box. I don't care if it doesn't do everything you need. Don't customize it and don't develop it in-house.

Technology is a tool. Do you go to the hardware store and ask them to make you a pink hammer with a special grip because you like pink and a standard hammer gave you a blister once? No? Do you need a toaster that automatically butters your toaster when it's done? No? Stop thinking of Information Technology as anything other than a standard tool, just because you can.

Yes... yes... it would be super cool if you email automatically dumped to a PDF for storage on your file server and then texted you a GIF of a dancing cat, but you don't <u>need</u> it. It would be super cool if accounts payables hand-wrapped invoices in gift wrap – but that doesn't add value.

Stop preventing value-added activities chasing something that makes your life a little easier or seems neat-o but doesn't add customer value. If your customer wouldn't pay for it, you wasting your company's resource with pet projects. **Stop investing in activities that don't strongly link to value.**

In War Story 6, the IT Department had written time tracking apps. If this company had the best time tracking app in the world, would they sell one more thing-a-mabob? <u>No</u>. Stop wasting a limited resource, your company's Geeks' time, on non-value-added projects like this. Buy a standard hammer and do not customize it.

<u>Don't reinvent the wheel!</u>

TYPE 5: KEEP AIR IN THE TIRES

You didn't re-invent the wheel, right? You are just keeping the air in the tires. Do it. Do the minimum maintenance to keep the tires on the bus.

TYPE 6: FLAT TIRE

If you have an opportunity to replace some custom unicorn, snowflake custom wheel that the Business People requested with a standard wheel, do it now. Otherwise, fix the tire.

TYPE 7: ALIEN INVADER

Any new IT initiative that does not deliver customer-value to the organization needs to be killed. Mercilessly. With fire. Now. It doesn't matter if it's the CEO's pet project or if it's 99% complete and it will be ready tomorrow. Kill it. Dead. Nuke it from orbit. It's the only way to be sure.

Any Alien Invader project that you complete will become a Mooch. Do you need one more thing to drain your time? You already have too many Melmacians in your house, drinking all your beer. You do not need more of that.

TYPE 8: THE MOOCH

Any existing IT initiative that does not add to delivering customer-value through a competency should be allowed to live, peacefully. Although it's a drain on the company's resources, someone likes The Mooch or it wouldn't still be around.

TYPE 9: MOOCH ON LIFE SUPPORT

Any IT effort spent on keeping the life support on is time and money thrown down the money-pit. You are bringing something back to life only to make it a Mooch again. Let the Mooch rest-in-peace. Have a wake. Bring tequila. Invite me.

98

CHAPTER 10: SO WHAT?

If you <u>actually</u> ruthlessly evaluated your IT prioritizes using C&A, **four things will happen:**

1. You freed up a bunch of money and Geek time.
2. You may have immediately eliminated some complexity.
3. You created a process to vet future projects based on contribution to customer-value which will continue eliminating complexity and future wrong investments.
4. As complexity reduces, the Geeks should drop out of firefighting mode.
5. Built a relationship between Geeks and Business People.

That's a huge win. Whew, That's it. Everything's better now. Thanks for coming.

The End.

You're still here? Good, because I was just messin' with you. That was just the first step. Remember. <u>There are no silver bullets</u>.

CHAPTER 11: MAXIMIZE FOCUS (BUSINESS PERSON'S VERSION)

So far, we've focused on:

- Defining your business's Customer-Value-Proposition (CVP).
- Defining your business's Value-Supporting-Competencies that create your CVP.
- C&A your IT activities with your business's VSC.

Next, let's identify the IT resources that the business needs to support the value-aligned IT activities. These are your value-aligned activities. Only these.

	Building Something New	Keeping Something Old Working	Fixing Something Old Broken
Strongly Tied to Competency	Type 1	Type 2	Type 3

Turn these into a list.

Things Strongly Tied to Competency
1.
2.
3.
4.
5.
6.
7.
8. Etc..

STEP 1: TALK TO A GEEK...AGAIN

Your Geek friend provided a list of things they do, either building something new, keeping something working, or fixing something broken. You've narrowed it down to identify which of these things help support your company's competencies, which in turn delivers customer value. Now we need to find out if your Geeks are equipped to do those competency-supporting, value-delivering things well.

This is going to be a sensitive conversation again, mostly because of the suspicion that Geeks have for nosy Business People. Geeks fear that nosy Business People want to slash budgets or fire Geeks. I wish that wasn't the general stereotype, but it is. We will fix that later.

As a Business Person, you likely have the emotional intelligence to handle this conversation, but here's how I would handle it:

> Me: "Hey Geek, I appreciate the help before. Thanks. I learned a lot. Man, you guys are crazy busy. I didn't realize IT was so complex. After our talk, I was looking at these projects on your plate and these ones seem like they could really generate some value for our customers." (Hand the list to Geek). "What do you think?" (Listen to Geek). "Do you have everything you need to get these done? I mean enough people, enough training, the right equipment, and enough support from the Business?"

STEP 2: IDENTIFY GAPS IN RESOURCE REQUIREMENTS

Hand your Geek this matrix and fill it out together. Remember, we are not giving the Geek work to do; we are trying to learn more about the IT Department and Technology. This is an opportunity to build a relationship and expand your understanding.

Things Strongly Tied to Competency	Enough Geeks	Enough Training	The Right Equipment	Enough Support
Project 1	Yes, No, or Maybe	Yes, No, or Maybe	Yes, No, or Maybe	Yes, No, or Maybe
Project 2				
Project 3				
Project 4				
Project 5...				

STEP 3: PUT YOUR MONEY WHERE YOUR MOUTH IS

Now, you, business Person, need to **step-the-up** and help resolve any areas where your IT department does not have the staff, training, equipment, or support to get the project done that adds value to your company. You are going to fight for your Geek like you are a mama Kodiak bear and that Geek is your cub, because otherwise you just read this entire book for no reason. Plus, if you don't help, you reinforce the stereotype that Business People don't care about IT. All talk, no action.

You don't have to get everything immediately. Find one project that is understaffed, under-trained, under-equipped, or under-supported and make a difference. Use all that influence you've accumulated as a leader in your company and get things done.

Follow up with your Geek and to make sure it happens. You both have some skin in the game because if this project is a win, you just proved:

1. You can increase customer value.
2. You can lead a cross-departmental initiative.
3. You can turn-around underperforming projects.

That's going to look amazing on your annual review, resume, and LinkedIn profile, right? Yeah, it is.

In Fix IT Framework, this is Focus & Resources (FR). You want to be focus, right? I think you have the potential to be the most focused at your company.

STEP 4: SAY THANK YOU

You are now going to say, "Good job" and "Thank you" to every Geek on the project. Individually. In-person. You are going to say, "You added a lot of value to the company by completing this project. This project

---

Why A Cup of Coffee Was the Best Leadership Investment I Ever Made

One of my senior system admins came in at 4:00 AM to help deploy some new app. He always had a Starbucks' cup on his desk, so that morning I bought him a cup of Starbucks, stopped by his desk, said "Hey man, thanks for coming in early. I know it sucks. Coffee's on me." That's it. No big deal. Three bucks & maybe 15 minutes extra to my morning commute.

Two weeks later, after I had completely forgotten about that coffee (and wouldn't have this story to tell except for this part), he came up to me and said, "You're the best boss I've ever had."

"Man, you must have had some terrible bosses," I joked.

He explained, "I've been doing this for 15 years and coming in early all the time. No one has ever bought me a cup of coffee."

That was the best $3 I've ever spent. Ever. Ever, ever, ever. And it was 15 years overdue.

say, "Thank You" to your Geeks.

---

supports {insert VSC} which creates {CVP}, which generates revenue from our customers. Good job."

STEP 5: ADVERTISE THE WIN

You need to tell everyone you see about the success of this project. Every time someone complains about IT, you need to say, "Man, they knocked this one other of the park," because of two specific cognitive biases called the availability cascade and fundamental attribution error.

A cognitive bias is an incorrect pattern of thought that human beings fall into that leads to wrong thinking. Everyone falls victim to cognitive biases. If you don't think you do, that's actually because of naïve realism, another cognitive bias.

The availability cascade is the tendency to believe things we hear repeatedly.

The fundamental attribution error is the tendency to excuse our own failures as circumstantial or bad luck but to blame other's failures on their character.

For example, when you get a speeding ticket, you were just keeping up with traffic. But when someone else gets a speeding ticket, they are a reckless driver.

By allowing people to continue saying negative things about the Geeks, you are reinforcing the blame cycle that fuels how broken things are.

You are going to be the person to stop it.

CHAPTER 11: MAXIMIZE FOCUS (GEEK'S VERSION)

So far, we've focused on:

- Defining your business's CVP.
- Defining your business's VSC that create your CVP.
- Used C&A to align your IT activities with your business's VSC.

Next, let's identify the IT resources that the business needs to support the value-aligned IT activities. These are your value-aligned activities. Only these.

	Building Something New	Keeping Something Old Working	Fixing Something Old Broken
Strongly Tied to Competency	Type 1	Type 2	Type 3

Fill out the first column of this matrix using Type 1, 2, and 3 activities and projects.

Things Strongly Tied to Competency	Enough Geeks	Enough Training	The Right Equipment	Enough Support
Project 1				
Project 2				
Project 3				
Project 4				
Project 5...				

STEP 1: IDENTIFY GAPS IN RESOURCE REQUIREMENTS

You need to be brutally honest in this step. If you fill this out like a kid in a candy store, you might as well throw this book away. Business People already see Geeks as a money-pit where dollar bills go to die. If you make a Christmas wishlist like you're a red-headed orphan adopted by a multibillionaire, you are going to have a hard-knocks life.

I'm not saying to understate reality. I am saying to be realistic.

You need to decide if you have enough technical people, enough training, the right equipment, and business support for this project?

Honest. No gold-plating.

Things Strongly Tied to Competency	Enough Geeks	Enough Training	The Right Equipment	Enough Support
Project 1	Yes, No, or Maybe	Yes, No, or Maybe	Yes, No, or Maybe	Yes, No, or Maybe
Project 2				
Project 3				
Project 4				
Project 5...				

STEP 2: TALK TO A BUSINESS PERSON AGAIN.

This is going to be a sensitive conversation again, mostly because of the suspicion that Business People have that Geeks just want more and more money. I wish that wasn't the general stereotype, but it is. We will fix that later.

You don't have to get everything immediately. Let the business Person pick one project that is under-staffed, under-trained, under-equipped, or under-supported. I don't care if you think it should be a different one. This is about showing that you can line up with the business and produce CVP. Don't argue. Don't interrupt. Don't critique, cajole, or convince. Let the Business Person pick and say, "Thank you."

As a Geek, you likely have the logical rational intellect to handle this conversation, but here's how I would handle it:

> Me: "Hey Business Person, I appreciate the help before. Thanks. I learned a lot. I didn't realize the business was so complex. After our talk, I was looking at my IT projects and these ones seem like they could really generate some value for our customers." (Hand the list to business Person). "What do you think?" (Listen to business Person). "Which one do you think is most valuable?" (Listen to business Person). "We could make this one happen better if we had (insert what you <u>need</u>, not want... need... to make the project successful. Could you help me get this one project off the ground?"

STEP 3: PUT UP OR SHUT UP

Now, you, Geek, need to **step-the-up** and get this project done like your life depended on it. You are run this project like you are running from a mama Kodiak bear protecting her cub because otherwise you just read this entire book for no reason. Plus, if you don't finish this on-time and well, you reinforce the stereotype that Geeks just spend money and don't care about the business. All talk, no action.

Update your business Person and to make sure you deliver. You both have some skin in the game because if this project is a win, you just proved:

1. You can increase business value.
2. You have soft-skills to work with a business unit.
3. You can turn-around underperforming projects.

That's going to look amazing on your annual review, resume, and LinkedIn profile, right? Yeah, it is.

In Fix IT Framework, this is Focus and Resource (FR). You want Focus & Resources, right? I think you have the potential to be the most focused person at your company.

STEP 4: SAY THANK YOU

You are now going to say, "Good job" and "Thank you" to the Business Person who helped your project. You are going to say, "I couldn't have done this project without you. This project supports {insert VSC} which creates {CVP}, which generates revenue from our customers. Good job."

STEP 5: ADVERTISE THE WIN

You need to tell everyone you see about the success of this project. Every time a Geek complains about Business People, you need to say, "Man, they really helped me on this one," because of two specific cognitive biases called the availability cascade and fundamental attribution error.

A cognitive bias is an incorrect pattern of thought that human beings fall into that leads to wrong thinking. Everyone falls victim to cognitive biases. If you don't think you do, that's actually because of naïve realism, another cognitive bias.

The availability cascade is the tendency to believe things we hear repeatedly.

The fundamental attribution error is the tendency to excuse our own failures as circumstantial or bad luck but to blame other's failures on their character.

For example, when you get a speeding ticket, you were keeping up with traffic. But when someone else gets a speeding ticket, they are a reckless driver.

By allowing Geeks to continue saying negative things about Business People, you reinforce the blame cycle that fuels how broken things are.

You are going to be the Geek to stop it.

Why A Cup of Coffee Was the Best Leadership Investment I Ever Made

One of my senior system admins came in at 4:00 AM to help deploy some new app. He always had a Starbucks' cup on his desk, so that morning I bought him a cup of Starbucks, stopped by his desk, said "Hey man, thanks for coming in early. I know it sucks. Coffee's on me." That's it. No big deal. Three bucks & maybe 15 minutes extra to my morning commute.

Two weeks later, after I had completely forgotten about that coffee (and wouldn't have this story to tell except for this part), he came up to me and said, "You're the best boss I've ever had."

"Man, you must have had some terrible bosses," I joked.

He explained, "I've been doing this for 15 years and coming in early all the time. No one has ever bought me a cup of coffee."

That was the best $3 I've ever spent. Ever. Ever, ever, ever. And it was 15 years overdue.

Say, "Thank You" to your Business People.

CHAPTER 12: SO WHAT, PART 2

In Chapter 6 – 9, we:

1. Freed up a bunch of money and time.
2. Eliminated some complexity (immediately)
3. Created a process to vet future projects based on contribution to customer-value which will continue eliminating complexity and future wrong investments.
   a. As complexity reduces, the Geeks should drop out of firefighting mode.
4. Improved relations between IT and the business

In Chapter 11, we:

5. Created a strategic analysis of the gaps in skills, resources, and support.
6. Identified a prototype project that we <u>will</u> deliver on-time, on-budget, and that works like a charm.
   a. Which will increase the IT-business credibility and trust.
   b. Erodes the negative stereotypes.
7. Further improved the relationship between IT and the business.

CHAPTER 13: GROUNDHOG DAY

I had used "Mind the Gap" to identify a soft skills deficit on my IT support desk. I had just implemented a new customer service training program on the support desk to improve the Geeks' soft skills. We had done daily training sessions for over a week, when my boss got an angry call about how a Geeks handled a business Person. I listened to the situation and agreed the Geek should have handled it better.

My boss snidely said, "I thought you were going to fix this."

I said, "Hey, did I mention that I started running last weekend?" My boss was a huge fitness nut. I continued, "But I'm stopping, because I'm still fat."

She said, "No! You should keep it up! It takes a long time for your body to change, but trust me, it will work."

I said, "So you're saying just because I don't see immediate results, that doesn't mean the process doesn't work? That I should stop expecting immediate results, do the work, and trust the process?"

After a few seconds of silence, she said, "I get it. Keep doing what you're doing. I'll handle this complaint."

You are going to do Chapter 6 - 11 again and again and again, like Phil Connors stuck in Punxsutawney, PA. You're going to repeat it until IT most of your IT priorities are aligned with your business's competencies and value-proposition. You are going to Do the Work (DTW) until Geeks stop talking negatively about Business People and Business People are going to stop talking negatively about Geeks.

Is it going to be fast? No! Are you going to stumble? Absolutely! But you didn't think this was going to be a silver bullet solution, did you?

CHAPTER 14: SILOS AND HOARDING

EMOTIONAL ATTACHMENT

In Section 1, we talked about Geeks who had an emotional attachment to stuff. We looked at a company that had an emotional attachment to an old program (War Story 1 and 5), we looked at a Geek who had an emotional attachment to old worthless computer pieces and parts (War Story 1, 2, and 3), we looked at leaders who had an emotional attachment to their control (War Story 4 and 6). Information silos and functional silos can also be an emotional attachment.

I'll bet you have emotional attachments to unhelpful things.

Here's how you know you have an emotional attachment. If someone asks why you do something or have something, do you talk about the present value it has or do you feel a need to give them the background so they can appreciate it? If so, it's emotional.

For example, if I ask you about a piece of paper with scribbles of crayons decorating your cubicle, and you say, "Oh... my daughter did that for me when she was two..." Emotional.

If I ask about the purpose of a meeting, and you say, "The founder of the company wanted to ensure that the CEO and the employees got together monthly to..." Emotional.

If I ask about the purpose of a meeting, and you say, "We exchange information about current projects." Present tense. Not emotional.

If I ask you about a piece of paper with scribbles of crayons decorating your cubicle, and you say, "That's my handwriting. It's a note I need for a meeting today and all I could find was a crayon." Not emotional. And maybe get a pen. And some handwriting lessons.

Unfortunately, over time, we become blind to emotional attachment to things and processes and beliefs. It's only when someone points out that we have an emotional attachment to something that we recognize it and when we recognize it, we respond.

That's often how I end up at your company. Someone with new eyes looks at the state of things and says, "This is broken. I'll call David. He can fix it."

RESPONSES TO EMOTIONAL ATTACHMENT

When animals are attacked, they fight, flee, or freeze. When someone questions your emotional attachment, it can feel like an attack, so you fight, flee, or freeze.

Emotional fight response is exactly what it sounds like. If you want to see it, snatch a cookie from a baby. Red face, screaming, tears, anger, balled up fists. Try to reason with the baby. See if that works.

Emotional flight response is moving quickly away from the conversation. Changing the subject. Removing yourself from the situation. Or if you're in charge, maybe you fire the person attacking your emotional idol. "They aren't a good cultural fit," you think. Because they don't appreciate the rich history of your organization. And they are making waves. About things that are above being questioned. But you wouldn't do that...

Emotional freeze is mental shut down. The person attacking your beloved thing or belief is still there. The words are there, hanging in the air, but you do nothing. You don't respond. If you stay still, they will go away. You will outlast them. Then they will leave you alone with your Preciousssssss...

DEALING WITH EMOTIONAL ATTACHMENT

You can't logic away an emotional attachment. You need to create a different emotional attachment. You can do that by creating a new vision to attach to.

A vision is simply a description of a preferred future.

Here's a simple example. Imagine you want to make a change. Let's say you want to get rid of a bunch of old computers that are piling up in a closet. Start with what it will look like when it's done and what you will do with the free space. Maybe, "Hey Geek, I was thinking about starting a mini-library of technical books that people could read during lunch. If we could clean up the closet with those old computers, so we could put it in there."

Now in all likelihood, the Geek will move his computers to a new location because he has an emotional attachment to the computers, but you asked for the closet cleaned, not the computers gone.

Maybe you approach it as "I found a nonprofit that repurposes old computers for underprivileged kids. I know we have those old computers in the closet. Could we donate those?"

It's hard telling what will work because it's emotional – not logical. You are changing hearts and minds, not solving math problems.

If there was a silver bullet to changing human behavior, I promise you that I would be the richest man in the universe, because that would let you rule the world. But you are prepared to try and try again because you are going to Do The Work (DTW) to figure out how to clean the problem up.

CHAPTER 15: INCOMPETENT LEADERS

Leadership is broken. As broken as IT is, leadership is a whole other ball of problems.

Here are some interesting facts about bad leaders:

- Most employees are unhappy with their leaders.
- Many employees would willingly give up their raises if they could fire their bosses.
- Poor management is the number one reason high-performers leave a company.
- Direct reports of bad leaders have higher heart disease, higher blood pressure, and higher death rates, but lower pay and lower performance.

That's broken.

Here's a good way to honestly assess your leadership skill. Don't look ahead yet. If you look ahead, you don't honestly want to know what kind of leader you really are. Answer these two short questions:

I think good leadership is:

(A) Pretty easy
(B) Not too hard
(C) Very hard
(D) Nearly impossible

As a leader I am/would be:

(A) Learning
(B) Sucky
(C) Above average
(D) Pretty good

Psychologists found an interesting cognitive bias called the Dunning-Kruger effect. It basically looks like this:

- If you don't know anything about something, you think it's pretty easy and you'd probably be pretty good at it.
- If you know a little bit about something, you think it's not too hard, but that you are probably above average.
- If you know a good amount about something, you realize it's hard and that you suck.
- If you know a ton about something, you realize it's almost impossible and that you are just learning.

Now look at your answers from the previous page. Dunning-Kruger. Hey, don't blame me for your answers.

I'm not going to fix your leadership problems in a chapter. There's no leadership silver bullet either. You have to assess where you are an DTW.

I will point out that in all six war stories to achieve meaningful change, the company needed to change someone in leadership.

> "Never attribute to malice that which is adequately explained by stupidity.
>
> Hanlon's Razor

It sucks because that bad leader is likely a good human being, put in a tough job without the skills to succeed. They just can't lead. I don't think they are evil. They are just incompetent.

Incompetent leaders can be fixed. It just takes a lot of analysis, self-reflection, training, coaching, mentoring, and feedback. Most people don't want to work hard at being a great leader. They will work hard enough to become a mediocre leader, but not great.

I remember a story about Michael Jordan and the phrase, "I want to be like Mike." The story told about how Michael Jordan would practice harder for longer than anyone else. Even after he was successful. The story ended with "Everyone wants to be like Mike, but no one wants to work like Mike."

There are no silver-bullets to greatest. And if you are a leader you have a duty to be great. Either that or get out of the driver's seat because

> "Never choose to be average."
>
> Rettig Family Motto

you've got the lives of everyone following you on that bus you are driving. Choose to do the work. **Be great or get out of the seat.**

Unfortunately, when someone is in a position with a lot of responsibility, the most expeditious solution is removing them. If your choice is one person or the entire organization, you need to put on your big boy pants and make the call.

Remember, if you have an underperforming quarterback, you replace the quarterback. If you have an underperforming team, you fire the coach.

And Mister or Miss C-Level executive, if you have one underperforming leader, that leader might be the problem. If you have any underperforming leadership team reporting to you, **you are the problem**. I've seen organizations where the CIO fired all of the VPs, because, "Every one of them was incompetent."

Sorry, buddy. You need to look in the mirror.

CHAPTER 16: ROLL CREDITS

I would love to tell you that every one of the war stories ended up with a happily-ever-after ending, but this is real life, I've been honest so far, and I'm not going to lie to you now. Here are the closing credits and a post-credit thought.

War Story 1: The First Geek

The IT department continued to make incremental changes. They made a couple of incredible hires and were able to address many of their technological deficiencies. Ultimately, the success of the new hires put a spotlight on an ineffective IT manager who was terminated.

One technical holdout was the ancient order taking system supported by the <u>one</u> guy who wrote it. When the President of the company asked one young Geek to learn how to support this old system, the Geek replied, "That sounds like a great opportunity… if this was 1970." It was hilarious. Over twenty years later I still laugh at that.

The company moved to a new location, the Geeks had established enough credibility to get the resources (financial and other) to enable the business to continue its profitable growth. It's still very successful today and I'm still friends with the people I met there.

War Story 2: A Geek Hoarder

USING PRIORITIZING TO REDUCE COMPLEXITY.

Minimizing complexity and eliminating the hoarding mentality streamlined department performance. The increased performance by the Geeks spotlighted a completely ineffective CIO. The company removed the ineffective CIO and brought in a better leader. During a severe economic downturn, over half the company was laid off, including over half the IT department, but due to a streamlined IT, the business was able to weather the economic downturn with a reduced staff. They recovered nicely and are growing again.

War Story 3: Can't Stand to Look at Them

Using Mind the Gap to Create Credibility.

I identified adding wireless and removing the internet limit as the two projects that would immediately gain some goodwill with the executive team. When the security Geek wouldn't remove the barriers and dug his heels in, I attempted to adjust his understanding, but ultimately removed him. It was tough because he had over a dozen-years with the company, a wife, and a child.

Afterward, I added wireless and removed the 30-minute internet limit which gained IT enough credibility that the once-tight-purse-strings opened. The Geeks made radical changes that enabled the company to expand into China and Mexico.

The IT team got moved back to the main office into a corner with glass walls facing a beautiful pond (sunlight!) and I implemented an open-office layout so that everyone on the team could enjoy the view.

At the Christmas party later that year, the president of the company said, "If you haven't been to the new IT area, you should go. Those guys are a blast to hang out with." Still one of my proudest moments.

I'm still friends with and mentor four of the Geeks from that job over a decade ago.

War Story 4: CEO Says Hop on One Foot

MINIMIZING COMPLEXITY TO ELIMINATE FIREFIGHTING AND ADD VALUE

I shut off all the email alerts and focused the team on the most critical servers. This immediately eliminated the firefighting mode and allowed the staff to try to solve the problems rather than deal with the flood of emails. This immediately decreased server crashes as we focused on fixing problems instead of reading useless emails. The incompetent IT Director lost his mind when the emails stopped, literally screaming at me in the middle of the office in front of my team. Then he quit.

The team, no longer firefighting, implemented software that automated server uptime (a value proposition). Ultimately, my team saved the company millions of dollars.

Unfortunately, I couldn't solve the micromanagement by the CEO. I left the organization in a better state, but not perfect.

Later, the organization faces multiple corruption lawsuits and filed bankruptcy which led to investigation by the government, more lawsuits, and a still-ongoing investigations.

War Story 5: I'll Build a Wall and the Geeks Will Pay for It

MAXIMIZING GEEK RESOURCES TO BUSINESS COMPETENCIES

I started attending business meetings and asked the two supervisors and the assistant director to join me. They refused.

I attempted to change the attitude of the Geeks; however, most of the department quit rather than work with the Business People.

I stay in touch with the best people I work with, reached out to them, and brought in some of the high performing Geeks with whom I had previously worked. I joked with them that they knew my standards and still wanted to work with me, so no complaining.

I asked the friend of the President for all his work to date, the friend quit the project, took the money, and ran. Coincidentally, the President retired shortly after.

My new team created a cloud-based application with self-service business intelligence reporting in under 9 months. The new cloud-based app increased revenue by $7.0M even after the $5.0M loss by the President's friend. Nearly five-years later, they still have a cutting-edge platform.

War Story 6: Blame Thrower

WINNING SOME BATTLES BUT LOSING THE WAR.

I started with minimizing complexity through prioritization; however, the CIO was unwilling to support any elimination of her applications, so I pivoted to increasing the skill level of the Geeks through education and training. The CIO did not see any value in external training, so I pulled some strings to get the CIO a free invitation to an exclusive CIO conference. She loved it so much she approved a budget for training the team.

The increased skill level of the Geeks improved the quality of the application; however, with the insane level of complexity the quantity of output remained below expectations.

The CIO continued to blame the Geeks for not working hard enough. I shielded the team as much as possible, but the CIO continued to shift blame. Several of the Geeks quit.

When the CIO eliminated telework so that she could monitor the team herself, even more Geeks quit.

Ultimately, I knew that with the CIO in place, the Geeks could never meet the expectations of the organization.

Fortunately, a former co-worker called about that time who said, "David, can you help me? My IT is broken..."

In closing, I won some; I lost some. But every time, the company was better for having followed this process.

Sometimes companies improve enough that they no longer want to do the hard work of analyzing, prioritizing, simplifying, and executing.

Sometimes companies want instant results.

Sometimes the existing people or Geeks are threatened by a process that undermines their position or power.

But sometimes, **we win. And for those Geeks, Business People, and Companies, I know that I made a difference. And you can too.**

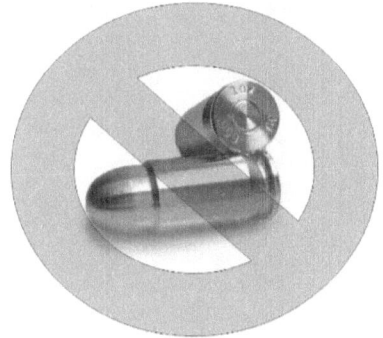

No silver bullets. Do the work.

129

APPENDIX: THE FIX IT FRAMEWORK

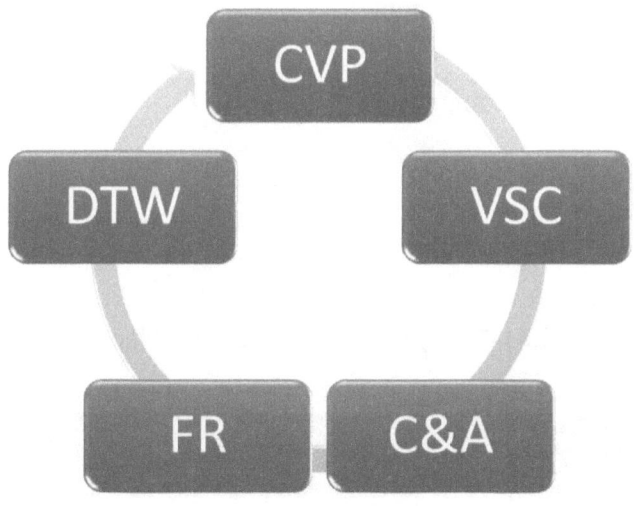

Define the Customer-Value-Proposition (CVP)

My business creates value for our customers by: _____

_____

_____

Then turn your CVP statement into a list of CVP Elements

Write down action-verb sentences that codify the CVP into individual statements.

1. My company produces customer value by _____.

2. My company produces customer value by _____.

3. My company produces customer value by _____.

List your Value-Supporting-Competencies (VSC)

Create a VSC for each CVP element.

1. How does your company do _____?

2. How does your company do _____?

3. How does your company do _____?

Classify & Assess (C&A) IT Projects & Activities and Place this Matrix

	Building Something New	Keeping Something Old Working	Fixing Something Old Broken
Strongly Tied to Competency	Type 1: Space Race	Type 2: Golden-Egg Laying Goose	Type 3: Constipated Goose
Might be Tied to Competency	Type 4: The Wheel	Type 5: Air in Tires	Type 6: Flat Tire
No Relationship to Competency	Type 7: Alien Invader	Type 8: Mooch	Type 9: Life Support

Focus & Resources (FR)

Pick one and do-it well.

Do the Work (DTW)

Make an organizational commitment to continue this process.

ABOUT THE AUTHOR

David G. Rettig has been married for 28-years to the only woman in the entire world with the patience to put up with him. He has three kids that think he's a great dad because they really don't know any better. There's a cat in his house who catches and eats houseflies. She may be a Flerken so he puts up with her. He loves weird people and weird things. He always tells his kids that everyone is weird, some people just hide it better than others.

David has a Bachelor of Science in Information Technology and M.B.A. from Franklin University in Columbus, Ohio, and a Master of Science in Management & Leadership from Western Governors University - Indiana. He's currently researching effective practices in leadership development as part of a Doctorate in business administration at Wilmington University, Wilmington, Delaware. He founded Rettig Tech, LLC and RettigVCIO.com.

When not compulsively attempting to become a better leader, David serves as the membership chair for his local Mensa group, contributes to the International Society of Philosophical Enquiry, and plays board games. His current obsession is Gizmos. Great game.

If you would like him to speak or consult with your organization on fixing your IT, you can reach him at **david@RettigVICO.com.**